CN00735539

# Natural Bakes

Everyday **gluten-free**, **sugar-free** baking

# Natural Bakes

## Caroline Griffiths

Smith
Street
Books

# Contents

Introduction 6

Cooking Notes 9

ONE
## Cookies 11

TWO
## Small Bakes 39

THREE
## Cakes 71

FOUR
## Celebration Cakes 103

FIVE
## Sweet Endings 123

Basics 143 · Index 154

Acknowledgments 158

# Introduction

Love baking? Me too. I enjoy the whole process and the buzz from the knowledge that I am making others happy with something I have created with love and care. If it just happens to have less sugar and be free from gluten, then even better. Without relying on sugar, the unique flavours of pure vanilla, nuts, spices and chocolate get their chance to shine. Not to mention vegetables, fruit and even the odd legume.

Being mindful of the ingredients we consume is one of the keys to a healthy life. Replacing store-bought, processed products with home-baked treats is a simple step we can take to help achieve this. Now, this is not a health-food book or a diet book; it is a cookbook filled with delightful, naturally sweet creations that are free from gluten and also happen to contain less sugar. Whether you're wanting to reduce the amount of sugar in your diet, looking to ditch fructose or cut the sweet stuff from your life completely, there are recipes in here to suit you.

I have avoided the use of fructose-containing refined cane (or beet) sugar (sucrose) and only used whole and dried fruits. Yes, fruit does contain fructose in its natural form, but you get the benefit of the fibre and nutrients as well. By 'refined-sugar free', I mean fructose-free, except for fructose from whole or dried fruit.

I have also created my own gluten-free flour blends – one ideal for cookies and biscuits; the others for cakes and pastry.

You will find a variety of recipes in this book, suitable for all skill levels and perfect for any number of occasions. There are simple biscuits, cookies and slices that make wonderful teatime and lunchbox treats; fancy cakes to impress all, suitable for any celebration, or everyday cakes and fruity loaves to be enjoyed at any time; small bakes that are great for feeding a crowd; and a collection of sweet endings filled with post-dinner treats. Some recipes do contain a few unexpected savoury ingredients, but don't be put off – I urge you to try them. The natural sweetness and textures given by these ingredients shine through and makes for a satisfying dish that is wholesome and filling. Please enjoy these natural bakes with your loved ones, colleagues and friends – they're not just delicious, but better for you, too.

## TYPES OF SUGAR

Carbohydrates, along with fat, fibre, protein and water, are needed for growth, energy and health. It is recommended that 50–60 per cent of our total daily energy intake comes from nutrient-dense complex-carbohydrate foods such as wholegrains, fruits and vegetables. Sugars are the simplest carbohydrates, the most basic of which are monosaccharides made up of single molecules and disaccharides (double sugars) consisting of two monosaccharide molecules.

### Sucrose

Extracted from sugarcane (and beets), sucrose is variously known as table sugar, white sugar, refined sugar, brown sugar, caster (superfine) sugar, icing (confectioners') sugar, raw sugar or sugar, among others. It is also found in fruits and some vegetables. Sucrose is a disaccharide, and the two molecules that make up sucrose are glucose and fructose – 50 per cent each.

### Glucose

A monosaccharide, glucose is the most plentiful of the simple sugars and is found in ripe fruits, some vegetables and honey. All carbohydrates except for fibre and fructose are eventually converted into glucose by the body. It is our primary fuel and essential to life.

## Fructose

Found in fruits, honey, maple syrup, molasses and agave syrup, fructose is a monosaccharide and is one of the simplest forms of sugar. Fructose and glucose bind together to make sucrose. Fructose comes under close scrutiny and it is the form of sugar we need to be particularly aware of.

Fructose is metabolised differently in our bodies; unlike glucose that is used by almost every cell, when fructose travels to the liver it is converted into triglycerides (fat) that circulate the body. When we eat more fructose than our bodies can manage (because we are not fully aware of all the 'hidden' sugars we are consuming), our livers become overloaded and we're headed for trouble. The consequences of too much fructose are complex, but put simply, it can contribute to loss of appetite control that may stimulate hunger and lead to overeating. It has been linked to fatty liver disease, cardiovascular problems (increased risk of heart disease and stroke) and type 2 diabetes.

## SWEETENERS USED IN THIS BOOK

### Natural whole and dried fruit

Whole fruit lends its natural sweetness and moisture to recipes. Homemade puréed apple adds bulk and texture where refined sugar has been removed, especially in cakes. Dried fruit adds pops of flavour and sweetness.

### Rice malt syrup

Also known as brown rice syrup, rice malt syrup is made by culturing rice with enzymes to break down the starches, and then cooking it down to create a thick syrup. It has a similar texture to honey and is less sweet on the palate. Unlike honey, though, it does not contain fructose. Try to purchase organic rice malt syrup. It is available from health-food stores and supermarkets.

### Dextrose

This monosaccharide is also known as glucose powder or dextrose monohydrate. It is made up of glucose molecules derived from grains and is less sweet than refined sugar. It does not contain fructose. I have used dextrose in its powdered form in this book. The texture is somewhere between granulated refined sugar and icing (confectioners') sugar. It is available from health-food stores, supermarkets (look in the sports drink aisle) and the 'brewing' aisle of some department stores.

### Monk fruit extract powder

Also known as luo han guo, monk fruit extract powder is, unsurprisingly, extracted from the monk fruit, a vine native to China and Thailand. It is up to 200 times sweeter than fructose, so you only need a little – usually less than a teaspoon – to make a big impact in recipes. It is my preferred sweetener. I find that it doesn't have the aftertaste that stevia has.

Don't confuse the extract powder with other monk fruit products that are bulked out with xylitol or erythritol and are used as 1:1 substitutes for traditional sugar (I don't use these). As monk fruit extract powder is sensitive to moisture, store it in a dry, airtight container and always use a dry spoon. The fine brown extract powder is available from health-food stores and selected supermarkets.

### Liquid stevia

Stevia is extracted from the leaves of the stevia plant that's native to South America. It is super sweet, so you only need between a few drops and up to a teaspoon per recipe. Brands do vary in strength of sweetness and bitterness. It is available from health-food stores and selected supermarkets.

As you integrate less sugar into your diet, you will find that your sweetness threshold lowers as your palate adjusts. If you do have a sweet tooth, you may sometimes be surprised by the lack of overall sweetness in some of these recipes – if this is the case, add a little monk fruit extract powder until you get used to it.

## GLUTEN-FREE FLOURS

Due to the unique properties of the gluten proteins found in wheat flour, there is no single gluten-free alternative that can replace it in traditional baking. Fortunately, by combining different flours and starches in blended mixes, taking into account their individual qualities, it is possible to achieve great results in your baking without gluten-containing flours.

Pre-mixed all-purpose gluten-free flours are readily available, but their quality can vary. Success cannot be guaranteed, and no one blend will work equally well for all recipes. I recommend making your own blend, especially if you are baking regularly. It will be more cost effective as well. I have created two blends that are used extensively throughout this book: #1 is ideal for cookie and biscuit baking; #2 is perfect for cake baking. I've also included a pastry blend.

Often, gluten-free flour blends can contain:

### Sorghum flour

Sorghum flour is slightly gritty in texture before baking, and has a subtle flavour and pale-brown colour. I love this protein flour and it forms the base of my cake and pastry blends. It contributes stability and structure to the crumb, plus flavour, texture and body. When combined with starchy flours if performs brilliantly. It is available from health-food stores and some supermarkets.

### Fine brown rice flour

Brown rice flour is the other protein flour that I like to use. Made from rice with the outer bran layer and germ included, it has a relatively neutral, lightly toasted flavour, with a slight graininess (try to find one that is finely ground). Like sorghum flour, brown rice flour lends stability and structure to the crumb, plus flavour, texture and body. Buy it from health-food stores and selected supermarkets.

### Potato starch

Potato starch is made from the starchy part of the potato only. It has a neutral flavour, with a light, silky texture. Starchy flours, such as potato starch, add lightness and airiness to the crumb, while softening the dominance of the protein flour (sorghum or brown rice flour) in a blend. You'll find it in health-food stores, some supermarkets and Asian grocery stores.

### Cornflour (cornstarch)

Made from the endosperm of the corn grain, cornflour is a flavourless and versatile starch. It adds lightness and airiness to the crumb, while softening the dominance of the protein flour in a blend. It is widely available.

### Tapioca flour (sometimes called tapioca starch or manioc flour)

Made from the root of the cassava plant, tapioca flour is soft, fine and bright white in colour, with little or no flavour. It lightens the crumb, while adding a bit of 'chew' to baked goods and encouraging a crust to form. You'll find it in health-food stores, some supermarkets and Asian grocery stores.

### Glutinous rice flour

Milled from sticky or sweet rice, despite its name glutinous rice does not contain gluten. It is neutral in flavour, bright white in colour and finely milled. It is great for binding and adding structure, as well as adding pliability to pastry. Buy it from the Asian section of the supermarket or Asian grocery store; it is sometimes called sweet rice flour.

### Teff

Made from the tiny whole teff seed, teff is a light and fine flour, with a light-brown colour and slightly nutty flavour. It is great with chocolate! It bakes to a light texture, creating a soft crumb. You'll find it in health-food stores and some supermarkets.

### Coconut flour

This is a non-grain flour made from dried coconut flesh that has had most of the oil removed. With a light coconut flavour and fine texture, coconut flour will absorb large amounts of moisture. It is readily available.

# Cooking Notes

## Almond meal

Made from ground, blanched, raw almonds, almond meal adds flavour, texture and moisture to baked goods, especially cakes. It is widely available from supermarkets and health-food stores.

## Baking powder

All baking powder is gluten free.

## Butter

All butter is unsalted.

## Chocolate and cocoa

There are plenty of chocolaty delights in this book. The chocolate flavour comes from cocoa, chocolate or sometimes a combination of the two. I like to use dark, bitter chocolate with a cocoa butter content of 70–85 per cent cocoa solids. It does contain a small amount of sugar. Dutch-processed cocoa has a darker colour than regular cocoa powder and a mellow, deep chocolate taste.

## Eggs

All eggs are free-range and extra-large (55–60 g/2 oz).

## Hazelnut meal

Made from ground, raw hazelnuts, hazelnut meal adds flavour, texture and moisture, especially to cakes. It is widely available from supermarkets and health-food stores.

## Measurements

All cup and spoon measures are level and based on Australian metric measures: 1 cup = 250 ml and 1 tablespoon = 20 ml (4 teaspoons). For best results, weigh your ingredients instead of using cup measures.

## Ovens

All oven temperatures are fan-forced. To convert to a conventional oven temperature, increase the temperature by about 20°C (70°F) or check the oven manufacturer's instructions.

## Xanthan gum

A corn-based thickener, xanthan gum is used in small quantities to assist with the structure of baked goods. You'll find it in health-food stores and selected supermarkets.

# ONE

# Cookies

*Cacao nibs give a chocolaty punch without the added sugar. I especially love their crunchy texture and slight bitterness. You can add chunks of 70–85% dark chocolate if you prefer.*

# Cacao nib hazelnut cookies

## MAKES ABOUT 24

100 g (3½ oz) hazelnuts
125 g (4¼ oz) butter, softened
115 g (⅓ cup) rice malt syrup
2 teaspoons natural vanilla extract
1 egg, beaten
150 g (5¼ oz) Gluten-free flour
    blend #1 (see page 144)
75 g (¾ cup) hazelnut meal
1 teaspoon baking powder
¼ teaspoon salt
55 g (⅓ cup) cacao nibs

Preheat the oven to 160°C/320°F (fan-forced). Line two baking trays with non-stick baking paper.

Spread the hazelnuts over one of the trays and toast for 5–8 minutes or until fragrant and the skins have loosened. Let the nuts cool slightly then rub them in a clean tea towel to remove the skins. Discard the skins and roughly chop the nuts. Retain the sheet of baking paper for baking the cookies.

Beat the butter, rice malt syrup and vanilla extract with an electric mixer until pale and fluffy, scraping down the side of the bowl as necessary.

Add the egg gradually, beating well between each addition. Sift the flour, hazelnut meal, baking powder and salt into the mixture. Add the chopped hazelnuts and cacao nibs and stir until well combined.

Drop tablespoonfuls of the mixture onto the prepared trays about 4 cm (1½ in) apart. Flatten slightly with a fingertip dipped in water and bake for 18–20 minutes or until just starting to colour around the edges. Remove from the oven and leave to cool on the trays for 5 minutes. Transfer to a wire rack to cool completely.

The cookies will keep for up to 1 week in an airtight container.

*These cookies are perfect for when you don't quite have the appetite for a slice of cake, but you still fancy a treat. They are slightly chewy around the edges and more cake-like and soft in the centre. The mixture is great to freeze in portions, and then bake on demand.*

# Carrot cake cookies

## MAKES ABOUT 20

125 g (4¼ oz) butter, softened
85 g (¼ cup) rice malt syrup
1 egg, lightly beaten
75 g (½ cup) coconut flour
1 teaspoon baking powder
1 teaspoon mixed spice
    (pumpkin pie spice)
¼ teaspoon ground ginger
100 g (3½ oz) pitted dates or fresh
    Medjool dates, chopped
1 small carrot (about 70 g/2½ oz),
    grated

Beat the butter and rice malt syrup with an electric mixer until pale and fluffy, scraping down the side of the bowl as necessary.

Add the egg gradually, beating well between each addition. Sift the flour, baking powder, mixed spice and ginger into the butter mixture. Add the date and carrot and stir until well combined. Cover and chill in the fridge for about 1 hour or until firm enough to roll.

Preheat the oven to 170°C/340°F (fan-forced). Line two baking trays with non-stick baking paper.

Roll tablespoons of the dough into balls and place on the prepared trays about 4 cm (1½ in) apart. Flatten to about 1 cm (½ in) thick and bake for 15–20 minutes or until just starting to colour around the edges. Remove from the oven and cool on the trays.

The cookies will keep for 3–4 days in an airtight container.

*If you're a fan of peanut butter, then these cookies are for you! Make sure you buy peanut butter made from 100 per cent peanuts.*

# Peanut butter cookies

## MAKES ABOUT 22

280 g (1 cup) crunchy natural
    peanut butter
115 g (⅓ cup) rice malt syrup
1 teaspoon natural vanilla extract
50 g (⅓ cup) glutinous rice flour or
    cornflour (cornstarch)
1 teaspoon baking powder
100 g (3½ oz) dark chocolate
    (70–85% cocoa solids), chopped
    into chunks
70 g (½ cup) roasted salted peanuts
sea salt flakes, for sprinkling
    (optional)

Preheat the oven to 160°C/320°F (fan-forced). Line two baking trays with non-stick baking paper.

Combine the peanut butter, rice malt syrup and vanilla extract in a large bowl. Add the rice flour or cornflour and baking powder and mix well. Stir in the chocolate and peanuts until well combined. Using your hands may make this job easier.

Roll tablespoons of the dough into balls and place on the prepared trays about 4 cm (1½ in) apart. Flatten the balls lightly with your fingertips to about 1.5 cm (½ in) thick. Poke in any peanuts or bits of chocolate left behind in the bowl, and sprinkle with sea salt flakes, if desired. Bake for 8–10 minutes or until just starting to colour around the edges. Remove from the oven and leave to cool on the trays for 15 minutes. Transfer to a wire rack to cool completely.

The cookies will keep for up to 1 week in an airtight container.

*I can't get enough of tahini. These delicious little morsels are reminiscent of halva, but without the sugar. If you want them to be more than a mouthful, by all means double the size.*

# Tahini shortbread buttons

## MAKES ABOUT 36

100 g (3½ oz) butter, softened
80 g (½ cup) dextrose
1 teaspoon vanilla bean paste
90 g (¼ cup) tahini
150 g (5¼ oz) Gluten-free flour
    blend #1 (see page 144)
60 g (½ cup) almond meal
½ teaspoon monk fruit extract
    powder
1½ tablespoons white sesame seeds
1½ tablespoons roasted black
    sesame seeds

Preheat the oven to 160°C/320°F (fan-forced). Line three baking trays with non-stick baking paper.

Beat the butter, dextrose and vanilla bean paste with an electric mixer until pale and fluffy, scraping down the side of the bowl as necessary. Add the tahini and beat until well combined. Sift the flour, almond meal and monk fruit extract powder over the mixture and stir until well combined. Knead lightly in the bowl with your hand to bring the dough together, if necessary.

Combine the sesame seeds in a small bowl. Roll 2 teaspoons of the dough into balls and flatten with your fingertips to about 1 cm (½ in) thick. Roll the edges of the dough in the combined sesame seeds and place on the prepared trays about 3 cm (1¼ in) apart. Bake for 18–20 minutes or until just starting to colour around the edges. Remove from the oven and leave to cool on the trays for 10 minutes. Transfer to wire racks to cool completely.

The shortbread buttons will keep for up to 1 week in an airtight container.

*Toasting and grinding the whole natural almonds gives these cookies an added dimension. I like them with no added sweetness whatsoever, but by all means add ½ teaspoon of monk fruit extract powder with the baking powder, if you like.*

# Toasted almond, coconut & chia cookies

## MAKES ABOUT 20

200 g (1¼ cups) whole natural almonds
40 g (½ cup) shredded coconut
1 tablespoon chia seeds
1 teaspoon baking powder
¼ teaspoon salt
1 egg, lightly beaten
1 tablespoon melted virgin coconut oil
1 teaspoon natural vanilla extract
¼ teaspoon liquid stevia (optional)

Preheat the oven to 160°C/320°F (fan-forced). Line two baking trays with non-stick baking paper.

Put the almonds on one of the trays and toast for 8–10 minutes or until fragrant. Transfer to a small bowl and set aside to cool. Retain the sheet of baking paper for baking the cookies.

Pulse the cooled almonds in a food processor until finely ground, then transfer to a bowl. Add the coconut, chia seeds, baking powder and salt and mix until combined. Add the egg, coconut oil, vanilla extract and stevia, if using, and mix until well combined.

Drop tablespoons of the dough onto the prepared trays about 3 cm (1¼ in) apart. Shape the dough into rounds about 1 cm (½ in) thick.

Bake for 8–10 minutes or until just starting to colour around the edges. Remove from the oven and leave to cool on the trays.

The cookies will keep for up to 1 week in an airtight container.

*The mellow and warm comforting flavour of brown butter works beautifully with pecans in this easy melt 'n' mix shortbread. Just like traditional shortbread, the fingers improve after a couple of days.*

# Brown butter pecan shortbread fingers

## MAKES 24

250 g (9 oz) butter, chopped
375 g (12½ oz) Gluten-free flour blend #1 (see page 144)
80 g (⅓ cup) dextrose
¼ teaspoon monk fruit extract powder (optional)
90 g (¾ cup) coarsely chopped pecans
2 teaspoons vanilla bean paste

Preheat the oven to 160°C/320°F (fan-forced). Grease an 18 cm × 28 cm (7 in × 11 in) slice tin and line the base and two long sides with a piece of non-stick baking paper, extending the paper about 4 cm (1½ in) above the sides of the tin to assist with the removal of the cooked shortbread.

Heat the butter in a small saucepan over low heat until the butter melts and the milk solids (the little specks that separate from the liquid portion of the butter) become a nut-brown colour and give off a delicious nutty aroma. Swirl the pan so you can see the colour of the solids through the foam. Remove from the heat and immediately dunk the base of the pan in a sink of cold water to stop the cooking process.

Sift the flour, dextrose and monk fruit extract powder (if using) into a bowl. Add the browned butter, pecans and vanilla bean paste and mix well.

Press the mixture into the prepared tin, smooth over with a spatula and bake for 25–28 minutes or until lightly browned and firm to touch. Remove from the oven and put on a wire rack to cool completely in the tin. Cut into fingers while still warm and still in the tin.

The shortbread will keep for up to 1 week in an airtight container.

*You can enjoy these cookies by themselves, they're that good. Ensure they are completely cool before filling, as they are delicate while warm.*

# Chocolate sandwich cookies

## MAKES ABOUT 24

200 g (7 oz) butter, softened
80 g (⅓ cup) dextrose
125 g (4¼ oz) tapioca flour (tapioca starch)
125 g (4¼ oz) teff flour
35 g (⅓ cup) Dutch-processed cocoa powder
½ teaspoon xanthan gum
½ teaspoon monk fruit extract powder

### BANANA CASHEW CREAM

150 g (1 cup) raw cashews
½ banana (about 60 g/2 oz), mashed
about 1 tablespoon freshly squeezed lemon juice

For the banana cashew cream, soak the cashews in cold water for 1 hour. Drain the cashews, rinse well and drain again. Put the cashews in a blender with the banana and most of the lemon juice and blend until smooth. Add a little more lemon juice or water to balance the flavour (it should have a slight tangy kick) and to get a thick, spreadable consistency. Transfer to a bowl and pop it in the fridge, covered, until required.

Meanwhile, preheat the oven to 140°C/275°F (fan-forced). Line three baking trays with non-stick baking paper.

Beat the butter and dextrose with an electric mixer until light and creamy, scraping down the side of the bowl as necessary. Sift the flours, cocoa powder, xanthan gum and monk fruit extract powder into a bowl. Add to the butter mixture in two batches and mix on low speed until just combined. Transfer to a clean work surface and knead lightly to bring the dough together, if necessary.

Divide the dough in half and roll between two sheets of non-stick baking paper to 6 mm (¼ in) thick. Cut into rounds using a 4.5 cm (1¾ in) cookie cutter, re-rolling the dough as necessary. You should get about 48 rounds. Put the cookies on the prepared trays as you go, about 2 cm (¾ in) apart. If you find the mixture becomes too soft to roll, particularly if the weather is hot, chill the mixture for 15 minutes or so to firm up and then continue.

Bake the cookies (in batches if necessary) for 15–20 minutes or until just firm to touch, with a little give. Remove from the oven and leave to cool on the trays.

Before serving, spread a little of the banana cashew cream on half of the cookies. Place the remaining cookies on top of the cream to sandwich the cookies together.

Unfilled cookies will keep for up to 1 week in an airtight container. The banana cashew cream will keep in a sealed container in the fridge for up to 2 days.

*A sweet cookie with cracked peppercorns may sound a bit unusual, but rest assured this shortbread has an intriguing and delicious flavour with a slight kick. I love to use Australian native pepperberries – they're sweet, fruity, peppery and bright in flavour. Fresh strawberries are a great accompaniment.*

# Cracked pepperberry shortbreads

## MAKES ABOUT 25

125 g (4½ oz) butter, softened
2 tablespoons rice malt syrup
1 teaspoon Australian native pepperberries or mixed peppercorns
125 g (4½ oz) Gluten-free flour blend #1 (see page 144)
40 g (⅓ cup) almond meal
¼ teaspoon monk fruit extract powder
dextrose, for sprinkling (optional)

Preheat the oven to 160°C/320°F (fan-forced). Line two baking trays with non-stick baking paper.

Beat the butter and rice malt syrup with an electric mixer until well combined, scraping down the side of the bowl as necessary.

Crush the pepperberries or peppercorns using a mortar and pestle.

Sift the flour, almond meal and monk fruit extract powder into the butter mixture, then add the crushed pepper and mix on low speed until combined. Pop the mixture in the fridge for 10 minutes or so, if it is too soft to roll.

Roll 2 teaspoons of the dough into balls and place on the prepared trays about 3 cm (1¼ in) apart. Flatten slightly with your fingertips and bake for 8–10 minutes, or until the shortbreads are just starting to colour around the edges. Remove from the oven and sprinkle with the dextrose, if desired, while still hot. Leave to cool on the trays.

The shortbread will keep in an airtight container for up to 1 week.

*There's something about the texture of polenta shortbread that I find addictive, and here the addition of Australian native lemon myrtle gives it a lovely lemony fragrance and flavour. I like cutting these shortbreads into flower shapes, but you can use any cutters you have available. If the dough becomes too warm and tricky to handle, place it in a sealed container and pop it in the fridge for 10 minutes to firm up.*

# Crunchy lemon myrtle & polenta shortbread

## MAKES ABOUT 20

125 g (4¼ oz) butter, softened

40 g (¼ cup) dextrose

1½ teaspoons finely grated lemon zest

1 teaspoon ground lemon myrtle

190 g (6¼ oz) Gluten-free flour blend #1 (see page 144)

40 g (¼ cup) fine (instant) polenta (cornmeal), plus extra for sprinkling

½ teaspoon monk fruit extract powder

Preheat the oven to 160°C/320°F (fan-forced). Line two baking trays with non-stick baking paper.

Beat the butter, dextrose, lemon zest and lemon myrtle with an electric mixer until pale and fluffy, scraping down the side of the bowl as necessary.

Sift the flour, polenta and monk fruit extract powder into a separate bowl, then gradually add to the butter mixture while mixing on low speed until combined. Turn the dough out onto a clean work surface and knead gently until smooth.

Roll the dough between two sheets of non-stick baking paper to a thickness of about 8 mm (⅓ in).

Cut out shapes using a 5 cm (2 in) cookie cutter of your choice, re-rolling the dough as necessary.

Carefully transfer the shapes to the prepared trays using a small spatula, placing them about 3 cm (1¼ in) apart. Sprinkle with a little extra polenta and bake for 8–10 minutes or until just cooked through and just starting to colour. Remove from the oven and leave to cool completely on the trays. They are quite delicate.

The shortbread will keep for up to 1 week in an airtight container.

*I wanted to re-create the gingernuts my nanna used to make when I was a kid. They were tooth-breakers, but in a good way. When you remove the white sugar and gluten-containing flour from these guys the texture changes, but I hope Nanna would recognise them. If it's any indication that they're tasty, my youngest child can't get enough of them. Please note that the naked glace ginger contains white sugar, so leave it out if you're sensitive to it.*

# Gingernuts

## MAKES ABOUT 20

280 g (10 oz) Gluten-free flour blend #1 (see page 144), plus extra for dusting

3 teaspoons ground ginger

1 teaspoon monk fruit extract powder

½ teaspoon bicarbonate of soda (baking soda)

¼ teaspoon salt

125 g (4¼ oz) butter, softened

115 g (⅓ cup) rice malt syrup

1 teaspoon finely grated fresh ginger

1 egg, lightly beaten

1½ tablespoons chopped naked (uncrystallised) glace ginger (optional)

Preheat the oven to 160°C/320°F (fan-forced). Line two baking trays with non-stick baking paper.

Sift the flour, ground ginger, monk fruit extract powder, bicarbonate of soda and salt into a large bowl. Set aside.

Beat the butter, rice malt syrup and fresh ginger with an electric mixer until creamy, scraping down the side of the bowl as necessary. Add the egg gradually, beating well after each addition. Stir in the sifted flour mixture and glace ginger (if using) until well combined.

Roll tablespoons of the dough into balls and place on the prepared trays about 4 cm (1½ in) apart. Flatten the balls with a fork dipped in a little flour to about 1.5 cm (½ in) thick. Bake for 13–16 minutes or until starting to colour around the edges. Remove from the oven and leave to cool on the trays for 5 minutes. Transfer to a wire rack to cool completely.

The gingernuts will keep for up to 1 week in an airtight container.

*Melting moments are a nostalgic favourite of mine. They've been given a new lease of life here with a delicious passionfruit cashew cream, which you can also use as an icing for cupcakes or as a cake filling.*

# Passionfruit cashew cream melting moments

## MAKES ABOUT 12

125 g (4½ oz) butter, softened
2 tablespoons rice malt syrup
2 teaspoons vanilla bean paste
190 g (6¾ oz) Gluten-free flour
    blend #1 (see page 144), plus
    extra for dusting
½ teaspoon monk fruit extract
    powder
½ teaspoon xanthan gum

### PASSIONFRUIT CASHEW CREAM

75 g (½ cup) raw cashews
2–3 passionfruit
2 teaspoons rice malt syrup

For the passionfruit cashew cream, soak the cashews in cold water for 1 hour. Strain the passionfruit, keeping both the juice and the seeds. You will need about 1 tablespoon of passionfruit juice. Drain the cashews, rinse well and drain again. Put the cashews in a blender with the passionfruit juice and rice malt syrup and blend until smooth. Add a little more passionfruit juice or water to balance the flavour (it should have a tangy kick) and to get a thick, spreadable consistency. Stir in the passionfruit seeds. Transfer to a bowl and pop in the fridge, covered.

Meanwhile, preheat the oven to 160°C/320°F (fan-forced). Line two baking trays with non-stick baking paper.

Beat the butter, rice malt syrup and vanilla bean paste with an electric mixer until well combined, scraping down the side of the bowl as necessary. Sift the flour, monk fruit extract powder and xanthan gum into the butter mixture and mix on low speed until combined.

Roll 2 teaspoons of the dough into balls and place on the prepared trays about 3 cm (1¼ in) apart. If the mixture is too sticky, chill the dough for 15 minutes until easier to handle. Using a fork dipped in a little flour, flatten the balls lightly to about 1 cm (½ in) thick. Bake for 12–14 minutes or until just starting to colour around the edges. Remove from the oven and leave to cool completely on the trays.

Before serving, spread a little of the passionfruit cashew cream on half of the cookies. Place the remaining cookies on top of the cream to sandwich the cookies together.

The unfilled cookies will keep for up to 1 week in an airtight container. The passionfruit cashew cream will keep in a sealed container in the fridge for up to 2 days.

*Roasting the cocoa adds extra depth to these rich and dark chocolate cookies.*

# Fudgy roasted cocoa cookies

## MAKES ABOUT 16

30 g (⅓ cup) cocoa powder
   (unsweetened), plus extra
   for dusting
200 g (7 oz) dark chocolate
   (70–85% cocoa solids), chopped
60 g (2 oz) butter, chopped
115 g (⅓ cup) rice malt syrup
1 egg, lightly beaten
2 teaspoons natural vanilla extract
95 g (3¼ oz) Gluten-free flour
   blend #1 (see page 144)
½ teaspoon monk fruit extract
   powder
¼ teaspoon bicarbonate of soda
   (baking soda)

Preheat the oven to 160°C/320°F (fan-forced). Line two baking trays with non-stick baking paper.

Spread the cocoa in a thin layer over one of the prepared trays. Bake for 20–25 minutes, stirring the cocoa every 5 minutes, until dark brown and fragrant. Transfer to a small bowl and set aside to cool. Retain the sheet of baking paper for baking the cookies.

Melt 100 g (3½ oz) of the chocolate and all of the butter in a small heavy-based saucepan over low heat. Remove from the heat and pour into a large bowl. Whisk in the rice malt syrup, egg and vanilla extract, then sift in the flour, monk fruit extract powder, bicarbonate of soda and cooled cocoa and mix until combined. Cover and set aside in the fridge for about 1 hour or until the mixture is firm enough to roll.

Roll tablespoons of the dough into balls and place on the prepared trays about 4 cm (1½ in) apart. Using a fork dipped in a little cocoa, flatten the balls lightly to about 1.5 cm (½ in) thick. Bake for 10–12 minutes, or until dry around the edges but still a little soft on top.

Remove from the oven and leave to cool on the trays for 10 minutes. Transfer to a wire rack to cool completely.

Melt the remaining chocolate in a small heatproof bowl set over a saucepan of simmering water. Drizzle the chocolate over the cooled cookies and allow the chocolate to set before serving.

The cookies will keep for up to 1 week in an airtight container.

*These biscotti are perfect for dipping into your coffee. They're really crunchy with a slightly savoury flavour due to the rosemary. Please note that candied orange rind does contain white sugar, so use orange zest for a completely sugar-free biscotti.*

# Rosemary, hazelnut & orange biscotti

## MAKES ABOUT 30

2 eggs, lightly beaten

115 g (⅓ cup) rice malt syrup

3 teaspoons finely grated orange zest or 3 tablespoons finely chopped candied orange rind

2 teaspoons finely chopped rosemary leaves

250 g (9 oz) Gluten-free flour blend #1 (see page 144)

1½ teaspoons monk fruit extract powder

1 teaspoon xanthan gum

½ teaspoon baking powder

100 g (3½ oz) hazelnuts

50 g (⅓ cup) pine nuts

Preheat the oven to 160°C/320°F (fan-forced). Line two baking trays with non-stick baking paper.

Whisk the egg, rice malt syrup, orange zest or candied orange and rosemary in a large bowl. Sift in the flour, monk fruit extract powder, xanthan gum and baking powder, then add the hazelnuts and pine nuts, and mix until combined. Set aside for 5 minutes, then knead gently to form a smooth firm dough.

Divide the dough in half and roll each half into a slightly flattened log, about 20 cm (8 in) long. Place the logs of dough on one of the prepared trays and bake for 20–25 minutes or until lightly browned and slightly spongy to touch. Remove from the oven and leave to cool to lukewarm on the tray.

When the biscuit logs have cooled slightly, cut the logs diagonally into 5 mm (¼ in) thick slices using a serrated knife. Put the slices in a single layer on the prepared trays and bake for a further 10–15 minutes, turning the slices over after 8 minutes, until completely dry (they will crisp upon cooling). Remove from the oven and transfer to a wire rack to cool completely.

The biscotti will keep for up to 2 weeks in an airtight container.

# TWO

# Small Bakes

*These brownies are dense, but not heavy. They're quite rich, so you won't need much to feel satisfied – the perfect match for a cup of coffee.*

# Brownies with coconut-date swirl

## MAKES 16

280 g (2 cups) pitted dried dates, roughly chopped
1 teaspoon bicarbonate of soda (baking soda)
250 ml (1 cup) boiling water
2 eggs
80 ml (⅓ cup) macadamia oil or vegetable oil
100 g (⅔ cup) coconut flour
3 teaspoons baking powder
cream or coconut cream, to serve (optional)

### COCONUT–DATE SWIRL

70 g (¼ cup) pitted dried dates, roughly chopped
125 ml (½ cup) coconut milk

Preheat the oven to 160°C/320°F (fan-forced). Grease an 18 cm (7 in) square shallow cake tin and line the base and two opposite sides with a piece of non-stick baking paper, extending the paper about 4 cm (1½ in) above the sides of the tin to assist with the removal of the cooked brownie.

Put the dates in a small heatproof bowl and stir in the bicarbonate of soda and boiling water. Set aside for 10 minutes to cool. Mash well with a fork.

Meanwhile, for the coconut–date swirl, put the dates and coconut milk in a small saucepan. Bring to the boil over low heat, stirring often, then remove from the heat and set aside to cool for 10 minutes. Mash well with a fork.

Whisk the eggs and the oil together in a large bowl, then whisk in the mashed dates. Sift in the coconut flour and baking powder and stir to combine.

Spread the mixture into the prepared tin and dollop tablespoons of the coconut–date swirl over the top. Swirl lightly with the tip of a small knife. Bake for 25–30 minutes or until just firm to the touch and a skewer inserted into the centre comes out almost clean. Remove from the oven and leave to cool for 10 minutes before gently lifting onto a wire rack to cool completely. Cut into 16 squares and serve with cream or coconut cream, if desired.

The brownies will keep in an airtight container in the fridge for up to 1 week.

*The cannellini beans are a surprising ingredient that lends a great texture to these blondies, which are very tender and moist.*

# Banana chai blondies

## MAKES 16

400 g (14 oz) tin cannellini beans, rinsed and drained
1 ripe banana, peeled
80 g (2¾ oz) butter, softened
3 eggs
50 g (½ cup) fine desiccated (dried shredded) coconut
1 teaspoon baking powder
1 teaspoon ground star anise
½ teaspoon ground cinnamon
½ teaspoon ground ginger
½ teaspoon monk fruit extract powder
1 tablespoon cacao nibs

Preheat the oven to 160°C/320°F (fan-forced). Grease a 19 cm (7½ in) square shallow cake tin and line the base and two opposite sides with a piece of non-stick baking paper, extending the paper about 4 cm (1½ in) above the sides of the tin to assist with the removal of the cooked blondie.

Whiz the beans, banana and butter in a food processor until smooth and creamy. Add the eggs and coconut, then sift in the baking powder, spices and monk fruit extract powder. Process until combined – the mixture may look curdled, but don't worry, it will be fine.

Pour the mixture into the prepared tin and sprinkle with cacao nibs on top. Bake for 20–25 minutes or until just firm to the touch and a skewer inserted into the centre comes out clean. Remove from the oven and cool for 10 minutes before gently lifting onto a wire rack to cool completely. Cut into 16 pieces and serve.

The blondies will keep for up to 1 week in an airtight container in the fridge.

*This is similar to the classic coconut jam slice, except this one is made with chia jam. It is slightly softer, but just as moreish. Try it with a drizzle of cream or a dollop of thick, creamy yoghurt for the perfect match.*

# Coconut raspberry jam slice

## MAKES 16

150 g (½ cup) Apple purée
   (see page 148)
100 g (⅔ cup) coconut flour
60 g (½ cup) almond meal
60 ml (¼ cup) melted virgin
   coconut oil
2 tablespoons rice malt syrup
2 teaspoons baking powder
2 teaspoons natural vanilla extract
2 eggs
90 g (1 cup) fine desiccated
   (dried shredded) coconut
80 g (1 cup) shredded coconut
420 g (1½ cups) Raspberry chia
   jam (see page 149)

Preheat the oven to 160°C/320°F (fan-forced). Grease an 18 cm × 26 cm (7 in × 10¼ in) slice tin and line the base and two long sides with a piece of non-stick baking paper, extending the paper about 4 cm (1½ in) above the sides of the tin to assist with the removal of the cooked slice.

Combine the apple purée, flour, almond meal, oil, rice malt syrup, baking powder and vanilla extract in a bowl and mix until a dough forms. Transfer the mixture to the prepared tin and use the back of a spoon to press it evenly over the base. Bake for 10–15 minutes or until firm to touch and golden around the edges. Remove from the oven and set aside to cool slightly.

Whisk the eggs until frothy, then stir in the desiccated and shredded coconut. Spread the slightly cooled base with the jam and sprinkle the coconut mixture over the top. Bake for a further 15–20 minutes or until the coconut mixture is set and golden brown.

Remove from the oven and, leaving the slice in the tin, place on a wire rack to cool completely. Cut into 16 pieces and serve.

The slice will keep in an airtight container in the fridge for 3–4 days.

*These are more like lovely little almond cakes than donuts, but they work really well in the ring shape. If rosewater is not your thing, leave it out and add a little more vanilla extract. Rosewater can vary in strength, so add it to taste, with some caution.*

# Almond, rosewater & chocolate donut cakes

## MAKES 12

melted butter, for greasing
4 eggs
115 g (⅓ cup) rice malt syrup
240 g (2 cups) almond meal
2 teaspoons baking powder
1 teaspoon natural vanilla extract
about 1 teaspoon rosewater
edible dried rose petals and slivered
   pistachios, to decorate

### CHOCOLATE GLAZE

100 g (3¼ oz) dark chocolate
   (70–85% cocoa solids), chopped
125 ml (½ cup) thickened (double/
   heavy) cream

Preheat the oven to 160°C/320°F (fan-forced). Generously grease two six-hole 80 ml (⅓ cup) capacity donut tins with the melted butter. (If you don't have two, don't worry, they will be fine cooked in two batches.)

Whisk the eggs and rice malt syrup together until the syrup dissolves. Stir in the almond meal, baking powder, vanilla extract and rosewater, to taste. Transfer the batter to a piping bag fitted with a 1.5 cm (½ in) plain nozzle (or use a large zip-lock bag with the corner snipped off) and pipe the mixture into the prepared donut holes (alternatively, you can spoon the batter in). Fill each hole about two-thirds full.

Bake for 10–12 minutes or until well-risen and just firm to touch. Remove from the oven and set aside to cool in the tins for 15 minutes. Carefully loosen the donuts and turn onto a wire rack to cool completely.

For the chocolate glaze, put the chocolate in a small heatproof bowl. Heat the cream in a small saucepan over medium heat and bring just to the boil. Pour the cream over the chocolate and stir until melted and combined. Set aside to cool and thicken slightly, if necessary.

Dip the cooled donuts into the glaze and sprinkle with rose petals and slivered pistachios.

The donut cakes will keep in an airtight container for 2–3 days.

*These cupcakes are super moist and chocolaty. If you feel like adding a pink tinge to the topping, squeeze a little bit of juice from the grated beetroot and stir it into the topping mixture. Soak and cook your own cannellini beans if you have enough time – you'll need 240 g (8½ oz) cooked beans.*

# Chocolate, beetroot & orange cupcakes

## MAKES 9

400 g (14 oz) tin cannellini beans, rinsed and drained

3 eggs

80 g (¾ oz) butter, softened

85 g (¼ cup) rice malt syrup

1 teaspoon finely grated orange zest

50 g (½ cup) Dutch-processed cocoa powder

2 teaspoons baking powder

1 teaspoon monk fruit extract powder

½ teaspoon salt

1 beetroot (beet) (about 175 g/6 oz), peeled and finely grated

### ORANGE AND MASCARPONE TOPPING

120 g (½ cup) mascarpone

2 tablespoons thickened (double/heavy) cream

1 teaspoon finely grated orange zest, plus extra shredded zest to garnish

a few drops beetroot (beet) juice (optional)

Preheat the oven to 160°C/320°F (fan-forced). Line nine holes of an 80 ml (⅓ cup capacity) muffin tin with paper cases.

Whiz the beans and one of the eggs in a food processor until smooth and creamy. Transfer to a bowl and set aside.

Without cleaning the processor bowl, process the butter, rice malt syrup and orange zest until smooth and creamy. Add the remaining eggs, one at a time, processing well between each addition. Return the bean mixture to the bowl and sift in the cocoa, baking powder, monk fruit extract powder and salt, then process until combined. Transfer to a bowl and stir in the beetroot.

Spoon the mixture into the prepared cases and bake for 20–25 minutes or until a skewer inserted in the centre comes out clean. Remove from the oven and cool for 5 minutes in the tin before removing to a wire rack to cool completely.

Meanwhile, for the orange and mascarpone topping, whisk the mascarpone, cream and orange zest until slightly thickened. Stir in the beetroot juice (if using) and refrigerate until required.

Spread the cooled cupcakes with the topping and garnish with the extra zest.

The cupcakes will keep, un-topped in an airtight container, for 2–3 days. Spread with the topping just before serving.

*The simple lime icing is great on these flavoursome cupcakes. If the weather is warm, you may need to chill the coconut oil so that it is solid. Or, if you fancy a banana-y hit, top them with the Banana cashew cream on page 24. Soak and cook your own chickpeas if you have the time – you'll need 240 g (8½ oz) cooked chickpeas.*

# Chai chia cupcakes

## MAKES 9

420 g (15 oz) tin chickpeas (garbanzo beans), rinsed and drained
3 eggs
2 teaspoons natural vanilla extract
80 g (2¾ oz) solid virgin coconut oil
85 g (¼ cup) rice malt syrup
2 tablespoons coconut flour
1 tablespoon chia seeds
2 teaspoons baking powder
1 teaspoon ground cinnamon, plus extra for sprinkling
1 teaspoon ground cardamom
1 teaspoon ground ginger
½ teaspoon ground star anise

### LIME ICING

80 g (2¾ oz) solid virgin coconut oil
85 g (¼ cup) rice malt syrup
about 1 tablespoon freshly squeezed lime juice

Preheat the oven to 160°C/320°F (fan-forced). Line nine holes of an 80 ml (⅓ cup capacity) muffin tin with paper cases.

Whiz the chickpeas, one of the eggs and the vanilla extract in a food processor until smooth and creamy. Transfer to a bowl and set aside.

Without cleaning the processor bowl, process the coconut oil and rice malt syrup until smooth and creamy. Add the remaining eggs, one at a time, processing well between each addition. Return the chickpea mixture to the bowl along with the coconut flour, chia seeds, baking powder and spices, then process until combined. The batter will look curdled, but don't worry, it will be fine.

Spoon the mixture into the prepared cases and bake for 20–25 minutes or until lightly coloured and just firm to the touch. Remove from the oven and cool for 5 minutes in the tin before removing to a wire rack to cool completely.

For the lime icing, whiz the coconut oil and rice malt syrup in a food processor until smooth and creamy. Do not over-process as the mixture may warm up and melt. Stir in the lime juice a little at a time, tasting as you go until you get the balance of flavour right. If the icing is soft, put it in the fridge until ready to use.

Spread the cooled cupcakes with the lime icing and sprinkle with extra cinnamon. If the weather is warm, keep the iced cakes in the fridge until just before serving.

The cupcakes will keep, un-iced in an airtight container, for 2–3 days. Spread with the lime icing just before serving.

*Traditionally, madeleines are enjoyed warm from the oven. These not-so-traditional madeleines are equally delicious warm or cool. Soak and cook your own cannellini beans if you have time – you'll need 240 g (8½ oz) cooked beans. If you only have one madeleine tray, don't worry, the mixture will hold between cooking batches.*

# Almond, mandarin & orange blossom madeleines

## MAKES ABOUT 20

melted butter, for greasing
400 g (14 oz) tin cannellini beans, rinsed and drained
3 eggs
80 g (2¾ oz) butter, softened
85 g (¼ cup) rice malt syrup
2 teaspoons vanilla bean paste
2 teaspoons finely grated mandarin zest
60 g (⅛ cup) almond meal
2 teaspoons baking powder
1 teaspoon monk fruit extract powder
2 teaspoons orange blossom water
dextrose, for sprinkling (optional)

Preheat the oven to 160°C/320°F (fan-forced). Generously brush two madeleine trays with melted butter.

Whiz the cannellini beans and one of the eggs in a food processor until creamy. Transfer to a bowl and set aside.

Without cleaning the processor bowl, process the butter, rice malt syrup, vanilla bean paste and mandarin zest until smooth and creamy. Add the remaining eggs, one at a time, processing well between each addition. Return the cannellini bean mixture to the processor, along with the almond meal, baking powder, monk fruit extract powder and orange blossom water, then process until combined. The batter may look curdled, but don't worry, it will be fine.

Spoon about 1 tablespoon of the mixture into each hole of the prepared trays and bake for 13–15 minutes or until just firm to the touch and browning around the edges. Remove from the oven and cool for 5 minutes before transferring to a wire rack to cool slightly. Sprinkle with dextrose, if desired.

The madeleines are delicious served warm; however, they will keep in an airtight container for 1–2 days.

*Beetroot and chocolate are great partners – the chocolate is grounded by the earthy flavour of the beetroot. You can add a handful of roughly chopped pecans or macadamias for crunch if you like to this tray cake, just stir them in when adding the chocolate, beetroot and apple. It's also lovely served with a dollop of thick creamy yoghurt.*

# Beetroot chocolate tray cake

## MAKES 16

80 ml (⅓ cup) vegetable oil
3 eggs
1 teaspoon natural vanilla extract
100 g (3½ oz) dark chocolate
    (70–85% cocoa solids), melted
2 beetroot (beets) (about 350 g/
    12½ oz), peeled and finely grated
1 large apple (about 200 g/7 oz),
    grated with skin on
100 g (3½ oz) Gluten-free flour
    blend #2 (see page 145)
2 tablespoons raw cacao powder,
    plus extra for dusting
3 teaspoons baking powder
1 teaspoon monk fruit extract
    powder

Preheat the oven to 160°C/320°F (fan-forced). Grease a 20 cm × 30 cm (8 in × 12 in) slice tin and line the base and two long sides with non-stick baking paper, extending the paper about 4 cm (1½ in) over the sides of the tin to assist with the removal of the cooked cake.

Whisk the oil, eggs and vanilla extract together in a bowl until well combined. Add the melted chocolate, beetroot and apple and stir to combine. Sift in the flour, cacao, baking powder and monk fruit extract powder and mix until combined.

Spread the mixture into the prepared tin and bake for 18–23 minutes or until just firm to the touch. Remove from the oven and cool for 10 minutes before gently lifting onto a wire rack to cool. Cut into 16 pieces and serve dusted with extra cacao, if you like.

The cake will keep in an airtight container in the fridge for up to 1 week.

*This tender and slightly crumbly slice is delicious with a generous dollop of thick yoghurt or cream.*

# Fig, prune & cranberry crumble slice

## MAKES 16

150 g (¾ cup) whole dried figs, chopped
110 g (⅔ cup) pitted prunes, roughly chopped
65 g (½ cup) dried unsweetened cranberries
125 ml (½ cup) boiling water
200 g (7 oz) butter, softened
2 tablespoons rice malt syrup
1 tablespoon natural vanilla extract
175 g (6 oz) Gluten-free flour blend #2 (see page 145)
1 teaspoon monk fruit extract powder
½ teaspoon baking powder
225 g (3 cups) shredded coconut
50 g (1¾ oz) almond meal
cocoa powder (unsweetened), for dusting (optional)

Place the fruit in a small heatproof bowl, add the boiling water and set aside to plump up for 30 minutes or until cool, stirring occasionally. Mash the fruit roughly together. The mixture will be quite lumpy with most of the liquid absorbed.

Preheat the oven to 160°C/320°F (fan-forced). Grease a 20 cm (8 in) square shallow cake tin and line the base and two opposite sides with a piece of non-stick baking paper, extending the paper about 4 cm (1½ in) above the sides of the tin to assist with the removal of the cooked slice.

Meanwhile, beat the butter, rice malt syrup and vanilla extract together with an electric mixer until creamy, scraping down the side of the bowl as necessary. Sift in the flour, monk fruit extract powder and baking powder and mix until combined. Finally, mix in the shredded coconut and almond meal. Use your hands to make this job easier if you like.

Spoon half the crumble mixture into the prepared tin and use the back of a spoon to press evenly over the base. Bake the base for 10–15 minutes or until lightly coloured. Remove from the oven and spoon the fruit mixture over the top. Sprinkle the remaining crumble mixture over the top, breaking it up with your fingertips and keeping it in small clumps.

Bake for a further 18–23 minutes or until lightly browned. Remove from the oven and, leaving the slice in the tin, place on a wire rack to cool completely.

Dust with cocoa powder, if desired, and cut into squares before serving.

The slice will keep in an airtight container for 3–4 days.

*Donut moulds usually come in tins that make six donuts, but if you don't have three trays, these are fine to cook in batches. If you don't have any donut moulds, you can bake these – as well as the other donut recipes on pages 46 and 60 – in a couple of standard muffin tins; they just won't be donuts!*

# Spiced pumpkin donuts

## MAKES 14–16

melted butter, for greasing
380 g (1½ cups) steamed and
    mashed pumpkin (squash),
    cooled
150 g (½ cup) Apple purée
    (see page 148)
3 eggs
80 ml (⅓ cup) vegetable oil or
    melted butter
225 g (8 oz) Gluten-free flour
    blend #2 (see page 145)
2½ teaspoons mixed spice
    (pumpkin pie spice)
2 teaspoons baking powder
1 teaspoon monk fruit extract
    powder
pinch of salt

### SPICE POWDER

40 g (¼ cup) dextrose
2 teaspoons mixed spice
    (pumpkin pie spice)
½ teaspoon freshly grated nutmeg

Preheat the oven to 160°C/320°F (fan-forced). Generously grease three 6-hole 80 ml (⅓ cup) capacity donut tins with melted butter. (If you don't have three tins, don't worry, they will be fine cooked in batches.)

In a bowl, whisk the pumpkin, apple purée, eggs and oil or butter until smooth. Sift in the flour, mixed spice, baking powder, monk fruit extract powder and salt and stir until just combined.

Put the batter in a piping bag fitted with a 1.5 cm (½ in) plain nozzle (or use a large zip-lock bag with the corner snipped off) and pipe the mixture into the prepared donut holes (alternatively, you can spoon the batter in). Fill each hole about two-thirds full.

Bake for 10–12 minutes or until well-risen and a skewer inserted in the centre comes out clean. Remove from the oven and set aside to cool in the tin for 5 minutes. Carefully loosen the donuts and turn out onto a wire rack.

Combine the spice mix ingredients in a small bowl. While the donuts are still warm (but no longer fragile), gently toss them in the spice powder.

The donuts are best served warm from the oven, but will keep in an airtight container for 2–3 days.

*Peas? Yes, really! We use lots of vegetables and fruits to add natural sweetness to our baking, so why not peas? They are unusual, but rather fun, I think. These donuts are equally delicious dipped in Chocolate glaze (see page 46). Garnish with frozen peas for added texture, if you like.*

# Baked vanilla & pea donuts

## MAKES 12

200 g (7 oz) Gluten-free flour blend #2 (see page 145)
2 teaspoons baking powder
1¼ teaspoons monk fruit extract powder
pinch of salt
140 g (1 cup) frozen baby green peas, thawed, plus extra to garnish
100 g (1 cup) almond meal
125 ml (½ cup) full-cream (whole) milk
100 g (3½ oz) butter, melted, plus extra for greasing
100 g (⅓ cup) Apple purée (see page 148)
2 eggs
2 teaspoons natural vanilla extract
1 tablespoon slivered pistachios

### AVOCADO COCONUT ICING

1 ripe avocado, chopped
1 tablespoon coconut powder
1 teaspoon freshly squeezed lime juice, plus extra if needed

Preheat the oven to 160°C/320°F (fan-forced). Generously grease two 6-hole 80 ml (⅓ cup) capacity donut tins with melted butter. (If you don't have two tins, don't worry, they will be fine cooked in two batches.)

Sift the flour, baking powder, monk fruit extract powder and salt together into a large bowl. Make a well in the centre and add the peas, almond meal, milk, butter, apple purée, eggs and vanilla extract and stir until combined.

Put the batter in a piping bag fitted with a 1.5 cm (½ in) plain nozzle (or use a large zip-lock bag with the corner snipped off) and pipe the mixture into the prepared donut holes (alternatively, you can spoon the batter in). Fill each hole about two-thirds full.

Bake for 12–15 minutes or until well-risen and a skewer inserted in the centre comes out clean.

Remove from the oven and set aside to cool in the tin for 5 minutes. Carefully loosen the donuts and turn onto a wire rack to cool completely.

For the avocado coconut icing, mash and stir the avocado until smooth. Add the coconut powder and lime juice and mix well. Add a little more lime juice to adjust the flavour balance and consistency, if necessary.

Spread the cooled donuts with the icing and sprinkle with the pistachios and extra peas. Serve immediately.

*The pumpkin adds lightness to these scones that you perhaps wouldn't expect, and the colour is striking. I am a traditionalist when it comes to making scones and believe you should rub the butter in with your fingertips. You can do this step with a food processor if you like; just don't process for too long as retaining visible flakes of butter helps the texture of the scones.*

# Pumpkin & fennel scones

## MAKES ABOUT 10

225 g (8 oz) Gluten-free flour blend #2 (see page 145), plus extra for dusting
3 teaspoons baking powder
50 g (1¾ oz) cold butter, chopped
2 teaspoons fennel seeds, roughly crushed using a mortar and pestle, plus extra for sprinkling
190 g (¾ cup) steamed and mashed pumpkin (squash), cooled
about 125 ml (½ cup) buttermilk, plus extra for brushing
butter or Raspberry chia jam (see page 149) and cream, to serve

Preheat the oven to 200°C/400°F (fan-forced) and line a baking tray with non-stick baking paper.

Sift the flour and baking powder together into a large bowl. Add the butter and use your fingertips to rub it into the flour until the mixture resembles coarse breadcrumbs. Stir in the fennel seeds.

Make a well in the centre of the flour mixture and add the pumpkin and buttermilk. Using a butter knife in a cutting action, combine the mixture until it forms a soft sticky dough. Add a little more buttermilk if the mixture seems dry.

Turn the dough onto a lightly floured surface and very gently knead and press the dough together. Using your fingertips, pat the dough out to about 3 cm (1¼ in) thick. Cut out the scones using a 5 cm (2 in) round cutter dipped in flour. Place the scones on the prepared tray so they're almost touching. Gently press the dough offcuts together and cut more scones as necessary. Carefully brush the top of the scones with buttermilk and sprinkle with the extra crushed fennel seeds.

Bake for 18–23 minutes or until well-risen, lightly browned and cooked through. Wrap in a clean tea towel to keep warm and soft. Serve warm with butter or jam and cream.

The scones are best eaten warm from the oven, but will keep in an airtight container for 2–3 days. Split and toast before eating.

*Use your favourite combo of seeds to sprinkle over these muffins. I like a mixture of linseeds, sunflower seeds and pumpkin seeds. The muffins are best straight from the oven, but reheat well in the microwave. For a little extra indulgence, enjoy with a swipe of butter or Raspberry chia jam (see page 149).*

# Spiced apple & cream cheese muffins

## MAKES 12

150 g (5¼ oz) Gluten-free flour blend #2 (see page 145)

55 g (⅓ cup) dextrose

3 teaspoons baking powder

2 teaspoons ground cinnamon

2 teaspoons mixed pie spice (pumpkin spice)

1 teaspoon monk fruit extract powder

100 g (1 cup) almond meal

1 large apple (about 200 g/7 oz), cored and diced with skin on

150 g (5¼ oz) cream cheese, roughly chopped

2 eggs

250 ml (1 cup) buttermilk

a mixture of your favourite seeds, for sprinkling

Preheat the oven to 180°C/350°F (fan-forced). Lightly grease a 12-hole 80 ml (⅓ cup capacity) muffin tin or line with paper cases.

Sift the flour, dextrose, baking powder, spices and monk fruit extract powder into a bowl. Stir in the almond meal, then mix in the apple.

Mash and stir the cream cheese and eggs together with a whisk until roughly combined (there will be small lumps of cream cheese remaining, which is what you're after). Stir in the buttermilk, then pour into the flour mixture and stir until combined.

Spoon the batter into the prepared tin and sprinkle with the seeds. Bake for 18–23 minutes or until muffins spring back when lightly pressed. Remove from the oven and cool for 2 minutes in the tin before carefully removing to a wire rack.

The muffins are best served warm from the oven; however, they will keep in an airtight container in the fridge for 2–3 days. Reheat before serving.

*This is my guilt-free version of a jam donut, disguised as a muffin. These are best served straight from the oven, but reheat well in the microwave. I find silicone muffin moulds work really well for these duffins.*

# Jam duffins

## MAKES 9

150 g (5¼ oz) Gluten-free flour blend #2 (see page 145)
2 teaspoons baking powder
1 teaspoon monk fruit extract powder
¼ teaspoon ground cinnamon
1 large apple (about 200 g/7 oz), grated with the skin on
100 g (1 cup) almond meal
180 ml (¾ cup) buttermilk
2 eggs
50 g (1¾ oz) butter, melted
2 teaspoons natural vanilla extract
2¼ tablespoons Raspberry chia jam (see page 149)

## CINNAMON POWDER

1 tablespoon dextrose
2 teaspoons ground cinnamon

Preheat the oven to 160°C/320°F (fan-forced). Lightly grease nine holes of an 80 ml (⅓ cup capacity) muffin tin. Use silicon muffin moulds if you have them.

Sift the flour, baking powder, monk fruit extract powder and cinnamon into a bowl, then stir in the apple and almond meal.

Whisk the buttermilk, eggs, butter and vanilla extract together in a separate bowl or jug. Pour into the flour mixture and stir until combined.

Spoon most of the batter (reserving about 1 tablespoon for adding to the top of the duffins later) into the prepared tin. Make a small hole in the top of each duffin with the handle-end of a teaspoon and add about 1 teaspoon of jam to each hole. Cover the jam gently with the remaining batter.

Bake the duffins for 15–20 minutes or until they spring back when lightly pressed. Remove from the oven and cool for 2 minutes in the tin before carefully removing.

Combine the cinnamon powder ingredients in a small bowl, then roll the duffins gently in the cinnamon powder and serve immediately.

The duffins are best served warm from the oven; however, they will keep in an airtight container in the fridge for 2–3 days. Reheat before serving.

*These little galettes make a rather posh afternoon tea. The amaretto in the filling is optional, but it does give it a bit of an edge. An orange liqueur would work very well too. If you find you need to re-roll the pastry, stack the pastry scraps on top of each other rather than scrunching them together. This way you'll maintain the layers that you have worked so hard to create.*

# Pear & chocolate frangipane galettes

## MAKES 6

1 × quantity Gluten-free rough puff
    pastry (see page 146)
gluten-free flour, for dusting
2 beurre bosc or corella pears
1 tablespoon freshly squeezed
    lemon juice
1 tablespoon rice malt syrup,
    warmed
crème fraîche or creamy natural
    yoghurt, to serve

### FRANGIPANE

100 g (3½ oz) butter, softened
2 tablespoons rice malt syrup
2 egg yolks
120 g (4 oz) almond meal
35 g (⅓ cup) Dutch-processed cocoa
    powder
2 tablespoons cornflour (cornstarch)
2 tablespoons amaretto (optional)

Preheat the oven to 190°C/375°F (fan-forced). Line two baking trays with non-stick baking paper.

Roll out the pastry on a lightly floured surface to about 3 mm (⅛ in) thick. Cut six 14 cm (5½ in) circles from the pastry. (I use a small upturned bowl as my guide to cut a template from card. Be careful not to squish the edges of the dough as you don't want to impede the rise.)

Gently transfer the circles to the prepared trays and bake for 10–15 minutes or until puffed, starting to brown and the base is cooked when you peek underneath. You should have lots of lovely flaky layers. Remove from the oven and use a clean tea towel to gently press the pastry to flatten it slightly. Set aside for 15 minutes to cool.

Meanwhile, to make the frangipane, beat the butter and rice malt syrup with an electric mixer until pale and creamy, scraping down the side of the bowl as necessary. Add the egg yolk and beat until combined. Sift in the almond meal, cocoa and cornflour, then mix on low speed until combined. Stir in the amaretto (if using).

Divide the frangipane mixture between the pastry circles and spread out evenly, leaving a 1 cm (½ in) border around the edge. Core and slice the pears very thinly and brush them with the lemon juice to stop them browning. Arrange the pear slices on the galettes so they are slightly overlapping. Bake for 15–18 minutes or until the pear begins to curl and the pastry is a deep golden colour. Remove from the oven and set aside to cool on a wire rack, then brush with the warmed rice malt syrup.

Serve warm or at room temperature with a dollop of crème fraîche or yoghurt.

# THREE

# Cakes

*'Chocolate cake' might be a bit of an understatement for this cake. Who would have imagined that a cake made with legumes could ever be this light and tasty? This cake has a sophisticated bitterness to it – just add a little more monk fruit extract powder if you would like a sweeter version. Soak and cook your own kidney beans if you have the time – you'll need 480 g (1 lb 1 oz) cooked beans.*

# Chocolate cake

## SERVES 10–12

melted butter, for greasing
100 g (1 cup) Dutch-processed cocoa
  powder, plus extra for dusting
2 teaspoons baking powder
1¼ teaspoons monk fruit extract
  powder
½ teaspoon salt
2 × 420 g (15 oz) tins kidney beans,
  rinsed and drained
6 eggs
1 tablespoon natural vanilla extract
150 g (5½ oz) butter, softened
170 g (½ cup) rice malt syrup
creamy natural yoghurt or crème
  fraîche, to serve

Preheat the oven to 160°C/320°F (fan-forced). Grease a 22 cm (8¾ in) baba or ring (or 20 cm/8 in round) tin generously with melted butter. Add a little of the extra cocoa powder to the cake tin, tilt the tin to cover the butter with the cocoa powder, then tip out the excess.

Combine the cocoa powder, baking powder, monk fruit extract powder and salt in a small bowl and set aside.

Whiz the beans, 1 egg and the vanilla extract in a food processor until smooth and creamy. Transfer to a bowl and set aside.

Without cleaning the processor bowl, process the butter and rice malt syrup until smooth and creamy. Add the remaining eggs one at a time, processing well between each addition. Return the bean mixture to the processor and add the cocoa mixture. Process until well combined.

Pour the mixture into the prepared tin and bake for 40–45 minutes or until a skewer inserted into the centre comes out clean. Remove from the oven and leave to cool for 10 minutes before turning out onto a wire rack to cool completely. Serve, dusted with extra cocoa if you like and a dollop of yoghurt or crème fraîche.

This cake will keep in an airtight container for 2–3 days.

*This is a classic almond cake with a mandarin twist. If mandarins are out of season, by all means substitute two oranges, although they will need about two hours to pre-cook. The mandarins or oranges can be cooked the day before you need them.*

# Almond mandarin cake

## SERVES 10–12

400 g (14 oz) mandarins (about 4 small), unpeeled
270 g (1¾ cups) natural almonds
1 teaspoon baking powder
6 eggs
115 g (⅓ cup) rice malt syrup
½ teaspoon orange blossom water
dextrose, for dusting (optional)

Put the mandarins in a small saucepan, cover with cold water and bring to the boil. Simmer for 45 minutes or until very tender, topping up with water as necessary. Drain, cool to room temperature, cut in half and remove any pips.

Preheat the oven to 140°C/275°F (fan-forced). Grease a 23 cm (9 in) springform cake tin and line the base with non-stick baking paper.

Whiz the almonds in a food processor until finely ground. Transfer to a large bowl and stir in the baking powder.

In the same food processor bowl, process the cooled mandarins, eggs and rice malt syrup until well combined and frothy. Add to the almond meal mixture along with the orange blossom water and mix until well combined.

Pour the cake batter into the prepared tin and bake for 50–55 minutes or until a skewer inserted into the centre comes out clean. Remove from the oven and leave to cool for 15 minutes before transferring to a wire rack to cool completely. Dust with dextrose, if desired, just before serving.

This cake will keep in an airtight container for 2–3 days.

*The combination of the vegetables and the coconut flour gives this cake a unique, surprisingly light, texture. It's important to note that coconut flours can vary in the amount of moisture they absorb – so, I suggest you add the amount of flour suggested in the ingredients list, then wait a couple of minutes to see if you need to add a little more.*

# Carrot, parsnip & cardamom loaf

## SERVES 12

6 eggs
140 g (½ cup) Apple purée
  (see page 148)
85 g (¼ cup) rice malt syrup
2 teaspoons natural vanilla extract
2 teaspoons ground cinnamon
2 teaspoons ground cardamom
½ teaspoon salt
125 ml (½ cup) melted virgin
  coconut oil
2 carrots (about 240 g/8½ oz),
  finely grated
1 small parsnip (about 120 g/4¼ oz),
  finely grated
about 50 g (⅓ cup) coconut flour
150 g (1 cup) pitted dried dates,
  chopped
1 teaspoon bicarbonate of soda
  (baking soda)
2 teaspoons apple cider vinegar
2 tablespoons flaked coconut
butter or whipped solid virgin
  coconut oil, to serve (optional)

Preheat the oven to 160°C/320°F (fan-forced). Grease an 11.5 cm × 21.5 cm (4½ in × 8½ in) loaf (bar) tin and line the base and two long sides with a piece of non-stick baking paper, extending the paper about 4 cm (1½ in) above the sides of the tin to assist with the removal of the cooked loaf.

Whisk the eggs, apple purée, rice malt syrup, vanilla extract, spices and salt together in a large mixing bowl. Add the coconut oil and whisk well, then stir in the grated carrot and parsnip.

Add the coconut flour and mix until combined. Set aside for 2 minutes to give the coconut flour a chance to thicken. The mixture should be quite thick and drop heavily from the spoon. Add a little more flour if the mixture seems too wet.

Stir in the dates and bicarbonate of soda, then finally, working quickly, stir in the apple cider vinegar.

Spoon the mixture into the prepared tin and sprinkle over the flaked coconut. Bake for 1 hour 15 minutes–1 hour 20 minutes or until a skewer inserted into the centre comes out clean. Remove from the oven and cool for 10 minutes before turning out onto a wire rack to cool completely. Serve sliced, with butter or whipped coconut oil, if you like.

The cake will keep in an airtight container for 2–3 days.

*The base for this light and summery tart can be made a couple of days in advance and stored in an airtight container. You can fill the base 3–4 hours before serving. Use any berries or summer fruits that are in season.*

# Lime cheesecake tart

## SERVES 8

125 ml (½ cup) thickened (double/ heavy) cream
250 g (9 oz) cream cheese, softened
2 tablespoons rice malt syrup
2 teaspoons finely grated lime zest
2 tablespoons freshly squeezed lime juice
2 egg whites
pinch of salt
250 g (9 oz) fresh strawberries, sliced
mint leaves, to serve

### LIME CHEESECAKE BASE

150 g (1 cup) sunflower seeds
115 g (1¼ cups) shredded coconut
2 tablespoons sesame seeds
2 tablespoons rice malt syrup
1 tablespoon melted virgin coconut oil
1 teaspoon ground ginger
1 egg white
¼ teaspoon monk fruit extract powder
pinch of salt

Preheat the oven to 140°C/275°F (fan-forced).

For the base, whiz the sunflower seeds and shredded coconut in a food processor until you have a coarse sand-like texture. Add the remaining base ingredients and process until combined and the mixture clings together when pressed with your fingertips. Press the mixture firmly into a 12 cm × 35 cm (4¾ in × 13¾ in) rectangular loose-based fluted tart tin, evenly covering the base and sides. Bake for 15–20 minutes or until lightly browned. Remove from the oven and set aside to cool completely.

Whip the cream with an electric mixer until soft peaks form. Transfer to a bowl. Beat the cream cheese, rice malt syrup, lime zest and juice until smooth. Transfer to another bowl and fold in the whipped cream.

Give the bowl of the electric mixer a good clean and beat the egg whites and salt until soft peaks form. Gently fold into the cream cheese mixture in two batches.

Spoon the cheesecake mixture into the cooled base and refrigerate until serving. Serve topped with the strawberries and mint.

The tart will keep in an airtight container in the fridge for 1–2 days.

*Baked cheesecake is one of my all-time favourite desserts. The ricotta adds lightness and the dates add a subtle sweetness.*

# Baked lemon cheesecake

## SERVES 10–12

1 × quantity Almond pastry crust (see page 124)

100 g (3½ oz) Medjool dates, pitted and roughly chopped

60 ml (¼ cup) boiling water

350 g (12½ oz) fresh firm ricotta

350 g (12½ oz) cream cheese, softened

3 eggs, separated

1 tablespoon finely grated lemon zest, plus extra shredded zest to serve

60 ml (¼ cup) freshly squeezed lemon juice

1 vanilla bean, seeds scraped

1½ tablespoons cornflour (cornstarch)

pinch of salt

figs, fresh berries or other fruits in season, for decorating

rice malt syrup, for drizzling (optional)

Preheat the oven to 160°C/320°F (fan-forced). Grease a 20 cm (8 in) springform cake tin and line the base with non-stick baking paper.

Press the almond pastry crust firmly into the base of the prepared tin and bake for 10–12 minutes or until just starting to brown around the edges. Set aside to cool and reduce the oven temperature to 130°C/265°F (fan-forced).

Put the dates in a small heatproof bowl and add the boiling water. Set aside for 5–10 minutes to cool, stirring occasionally. Whiz the soaked dates, including their soaking water, in a food processor until smooth. Add the ricotta, cream cheese, egg yolks, lemon zest and juice and vanilla seeds, and process until smooth. Sprinkle over the cornflour and whiz again until combined. Spoon the mixture into a large bowl. Beat the egg whites and salt with an electric mixer until soft peaks form. Gently fold into the cheese mixture in two batches.

Pour the mixture over the prepared base and bake for 30–35 minutes or until lightly browned and the centre is just set – it should wobble slightly. Turn off the oven and leave to cool with the door closed for 1 hour. Chill in the fridge for 3 hours or overnight.

Remove from the tin. Just before serving, top the cheesecake with the figs, berries or fruits of your choice, and drizzle with rice malt syrup if you like.

The cheesecake will keep in an airtight container in the fridge for 2–3 days.

*This cheesecake is perfect for peanut fans, with its peanut butter swirl and chocolaty peanut base. Make sure you give the peanut butter a good stir before measuring it out, as the oil and peanuts tend to separate in natural peanut butter.*

# Peanut butter swirl cheesecake

## SERVES 10–12

500 g (1 lb 2 oz) cream cheese, softened
2 tablespoons rice malt syrup
1 teaspoon monk fruit extract powder (optional)
190 g (⅔ cup) natural crunchy peanut butter
60 ml (¼ cup) coconut milk
2 eggs
2 tablespoons salted roasted peanuts

### PEANUT BUTTER CHEESECAKE BASE

150 g (1 cup) salted roasted peanuts
115 g (1¼ cups) shredded coconut
2 tablespoons Dutch-processed cocoa powder
2 tablespoons rice malt syrup
30 g (1 oz) butter, melted

Grease a 23 cm (9 in) springform cake tin and line the base with non-stick baking paper.

For the base, whiz the peanuts and shredded coconut in a food processor until you have a coarse sand-like texture. Add the remaining ingredients and process until combined and the mixture clings together when pressed with your fingertips. Press the mixture firmly and evenly into the base of the prepared tin, and pop it in the fridge until required.

Preheat the oven to 140°C/275°F (fan-forced).

Beat the cream cheese, rice malt syrup, monk fruit extract powder (if using) and half the peanut butter (reserving the remaining peanut butter to swirl through the top) with an electric mixer until smooth. Add the coconut milk and beat again until combined. Add the eggs one at a time, beating well between each addition. Pour the mixture over the cheesecake base.

Gently soften the remaining peanut butter in a small saucepan over low heat or in the microwave. Place dollops of the peanut butter on top of the cheesecake and swirl it through the cheese mixture with the tip of a small knife. Sprinkle over the peanuts.

Bake for 25–30 minutes or until the centre is just set – it should wobble slightly. Turn off the oven and leave to cool with the door closed for 1 hour. Chill in the fridge for 3 hours or overnight. Remove from the tin and place on a serving plate.

The cheesecake will keep in an airtight container in the fridge for 2–3 days.

*This crustless cheesecake is a real treat with few ingredients. The cookies crumbled over the top add a great crunch and the blueberries add a touch of sweetness. You can also use fruits such as cherries or raspberries instead of the blueberries.*

# Cookies & cream blueberry cheesecake

## SERVES 12–16

500 g (1 lb 2 oz) cream cheese, softened
2 teaspoons vanilla bean paste
2 eggs
80 g (⅓ cup) sour cream
3 teaspoons cornflour (cornstarch)
1 teaspoon monk fruit extract powder
5 Cacao nib hazelnut cookies (see page 12), broken into chunks
125 g (4½ oz) fresh or frozen blueberries

Preheat the oven to 140°C/275°F (fan-forced). Grease and line the base and two long sides of a 17 cm × 26 cm (6¾ in × 10¼ in) slice tin with a piece of non-stick baking paper, extending the paper about 4 cm (1½ in) above the sides of the tin to assist with the removal of the cooked cheesecake.

Whiz the cream cheese and vanilla bean paste in a food processor until smooth. Add the eggs, sour cream, cornflour and monk fruit extract powder and process until well combined.

Pour the mixture into the prepared tin and sprinkle over the cookie chunks and blueberries. Bake for 30–35 minutes, or until the top is lightly browned and the centre is just set – it should wobble slightly. Chill in the fridge for 2 hours or until ready to serve.

The cheesecake will keep in an airtight container in the fridge for 2–3 days.

*This sweet potato and macadamia cream cake makes a great dessert, but really, there's no need to save it for a special after-dinner occasion – I keep coming back for a sneaky slice every time I have a cup of tea. You will need to start this cake a few hours before you need it, as the macadamias are best soaked for a couple of hours to soften them slightly before blending for the vanilla cream.*

# Chocolaty sweet potato & macadamia cream cake

## SERVES 10–12

1 large orange sweet potato (about
    420 g/15 oz), peeled and chopped
75 g (2¾ oz) Gluten-free flour
    blend #2 (see page 145)
50 g (½ cup) cocoa powder
    (unsweetened)
1 teaspoon baking powder
½ teaspoon bicarbonate of soda
    (baking soda)
115 g (⅓ cup) rice malt syrup
100 g (3½ oz) butter, melted
150 g (½ cup) Apple purée
    (see page 148)
2 teaspoons natural vanilla extract
3 eggs
1 teaspoon apple cider vinegar
Dutch-processed cocoa powder,
    for dusting

To make the macadamia vanilla cream, soak the macadamias in cold water for about 2 hours, to soften slightly. Drain and rinse well. Place 60 ml (¼ cup) of the coconut milk, the rice malt syrup, coconut oil, vanilla extract and finally the macadamias in a blender and blend until smooth, stopping occasionally to scrape down the sides of the blender, if required. Add a little more coconut milk if needed to keep the mixture moving – but not too much as the mixture should be quite thick and creamy. Transfer to a bowl and refrigerate until required.

Steam or microwave the sweet potato until tender. Drain, mash and set aside to cool. You will need 260 g (1 cup) of sweet potato for this cake.

Preheat the oven to 160°C/320°F (fan-forced). Grease a 20 cm (8 in) cake tin and line the base with non-stick baking paper.

Sift the flour, cocoa powder, baking powder and bicarbonate of soda into a bowl. In another bowl, whisk the rice malt syrup and butter until combined, then whisk in the sweet potato, apple purée and vanilla extract. Whisk the flour mixture into the sweet potato mixture alternately with the eggs until combined.

## MACADAMIA VANILLA CREAM

150 g (1 cup) macadamias
about 80 ml (⅓ cup) coconut milk
1 tablespoon rice malt syrup
1 tablespoon melted virgin
    coconut oil
3 teaspoons natural vanilla extract

Working quickly, stir the vinegar into the mixture and immediately spoon it into the prepared tin. Bake for 35–40 minutes or until just firm to the touch and a skewer inserted into the centre comes out clean. Remove from the oven and cool for 10 minutes before turning out onto a wire rack to cool completely.

Slice the cooled cake in half horizontally using a long serrated knife. Place the bottom layer on a serving plate or cake stand and spread with the macadamia vanilla cream. Top with the remaining cake half, dust with cocoa powder and serve.

The cake will keep in an airtight container in the fridge for 2–3 days.

*I know this is another chocolate cake, but it is quite different from the one on page 72, which has a more fudgy texture. This version is lighter but no less delicious. You'll notice the icing on this cake has a slightly grainy appearance. This is because the size of the dextrose crystals is not as fine as icing sugar. You can blend the dextrose to make it finer, if you like.*

# Everyday chocolate cake

## SERVES ABOUT 20

250 g (9 oz) butter, chopped
200 g (7 oz) dark chocolate
 (70–85% cocoa solids)
115 g (⅓ cup) rice malt syrup
150 g (½ cup) Apple purée
 (see page 148)
3 eggs
125 ml (½ cup) buttermilk
150 g (5¼ oz) Gluten-free flour
 blend #2 (see page 145)
50 g (½ cup) cocoa powder
 (unsweetened)
2 teaspoons baking powder
2 teaspoons instant coffee powder
¼ teaspoon bicarbonate of soda
 (baking soda)
cream, to serve (optional)

## CHOCOLATE ICING

100 g (3½ oz) butter, softened
240 g (1¼ cups) dextrose
25 g (¼ cup) Dutch-processed
 cocoa powder
80 ml (⅓ cup) milk

Preheat the oven to 160°C/320°F (fan-forced). Grease two 20 cm (8 in) cake tins and line the bases with non-stick baking paper.

Melt the butter, chocolate and rice malt syrup in a saucepan over low heat, stirring occasionally. Remove from the heat and transfer to a large bowl.

Whisk the apple purée into the chocolate mixture, followed by the eggs and then the buttermilk. Sift in the flour, cocoa powder, baking powder, coffee powder and bicarbonate of soda and stir until combined.

Divide the mixture evenly between the prepared tins and bake for 18–20 minutes or until a skewer inserted into the centre comes out clean. Remove from the oven and leave to cool for 10 minutes before turning out onto a wire rack to cool completely.

For the chocolate icing, beat the butter with an electric mixer until pale, light and fluffy. Sift together the dextrose and cocoa powder. Add half of this mixture to the butter, and beat until well combined. Slowly add the milk and the remaining dextrose mixture, beating until the icing is light and fluffy. Add a little more milk if required, to get a spreadable consistency.

Put one cake on a serving plate and spread just under half of the chocolate icing on top. Place the remaining cake on top and cover with the remaining icing.

The cake will keep in an airtight container for 2–3 days.

*First, decide which citrus fruit you have in abundance – limes, lemons, oranges, cumquats? Second, make this delicious cake.*

# Coconut cake with citrus syrup

## SERVES 10–12

150 g (5¼ oz) Gluten-free flour blend #2 (see page 145)
90 g (1 cup) fine desiccated (dried shredded) coconut
3 teaspoons monk fruit extract powder
2 teaspoons baking powder
4 eggs
100 g (⅓ cup) Apple purée (see page 148)
100 g (3½ oz) butter, melted
2 teaspoons finely grated citrus zest
pinch of salt
creamy natural yoghurt or cream, to serve (optional)

### CITRUS SYRUP

85 g (¼ cup) rice malt syrup
125 ml (½ cup) freshly squeezed citrus juice

Preheat the oven to 160°C/320°F (fan-forced). Grease a deep 18 cm (7 in) cake tin and line the base with non-stick baking paper.

Whisk the flour, desiccated coconut, monk fruit extract powder and baking powder together in a large mixing bowl. Separate two of the eggs and put the whites in the bowl of an electric mixer and set aside. Add the yolks, remaining eggs, apple purée, butter and citrus zest to the dry ingredients and mix until combined.

Beat the egg whites with the salt just until firm peaks form. Fold half of the egg white into the cake batter until combined. Add the remaining egg white and gently fold into the mixture until combined. Spread the batter into the prepared tin. Bake for 30–35 minutes or until a skewer inserted into the centre comes out clean. Remove from the oven and leave to cool for 5 minutes before transferring to a serving plate with a rim.

For the citrus syrup, combine the rice malt syrup, citrus juice and 1 tablespoon of water in a small bowl and stir until the syrup dissolves. Poke lots of holes in the cake with a skewer and slowly pour about half of the syrup over the cake. Serve warm or cold, with the remaining syrup and a dollop of creamy yoghurt or cream on the side.

The cake will keep in an airtight container for 2–3 days.

*The sweet potato gives this cake a slight sweetness and great texture, and helps to keep it moist. You can serve it with the Citrus syrup on page 90 if you like, but I quite like it as it comes, or with a dollop of creamy Greek-style yoghurt on the side.*

# Sweet potato, lime & poppy seed cake

SERVES 10–12

1 orange sweet potato (about 400 g/14 oz), peeled and chopped into 2 cm (¾ in) cubes

150 g (5¼ oz) Gluten-free flour blend #2 (see page 145), plus extra for dusting

75 g (2¾ oz) almond meal

3 teaspoons baking powder

2 teaspoons monk fruit extract powder

40 g (¼ cup) poppy seeds

125 g (4½ oz) butter, softened, plus extra for greasing

80 g (¼ cup) dextrose, plus extra for dusting (optional)

2 teaspoons finely grated lime zest

3 eggs

125 ml (½ cup) buttermilk

Steam or microwave the sweet potato for 15–20 minutes until tender. Drain, mash and set aside to cool. You will need 260 g (1 cup) mashed sweet potato for this cake.

Preheat the oven to 160°C/320°F (fan-forced). Grease a 22 cm (8¾ in) baba or ring (or 20 cm/8 in round or heart) tin generously with butter. Add the extra flour to the cake tin, tilt the tin to coat the inside with the flour, then tip out the excess.

Sift the flour, almond meal, baking powder and monk fruit extract powder into a large bowl. Stir in the poppy seeds and set aside.

Beat the butter, dextrose and lime zest with an electric mixer until pale and fluffy, scraping down the side of the bowl, as necessary. Add the eggs one at a time, beating well between each addition, then stir in the sweet potato. In two batches, stir in the flour mixture and buttermilk until combined.

Spread the mixture into the prepared tin and bake for 35–40 minutes or until a skewer inserted into the centre comes out clean. Remove from the oven and leave to cool for 2 minutes before turning out onto a wire rack to cool completely. Serve, dusted with extra dextrose if you like.

The cake will keep in an airtight container for 2–3 days.

*I love that all the sweetness in this moist and tender cake comes from the fruit, so you don't even need a replacement for sugar. I keep a stock of overripe bananas in my freezer for baking – when they've gone past the point of no return for eating, peel and place in a sealed container and pop them in the freezer. They'll keep for 4–6 weeks.*

# Hummingbird cake

## SERVES 16

200 g (7 oz) Gluten-free flour
   blend #2 (see page 145)
65 g (2¼ oz) almond meal
3 teaspoons baking powder
2 teaspoons ground cinnamon
440 g (15½ oz) tin crushed pineapple
   in natural juice
2 large overripe bananas, mashed
100 g (⅓ cup) Apple purée
   (see page 148)
60 ml (¼ cup) fresh passionfruit pulp
   (about 3 plump passionfruit)
2 eggs
150 g (5½ oz) butter, melted
20 g (⅓ cup) flaked coconut

Preheat the oven to 160°C/320°F (fan-forced). Grease a 20 cm × 30 cm (8 in × 12 in) shallow cake tin and line the base and two long sides with a piece of non-stick baking paper, extending the paper about 4 cm (1½ in) above the sides of the tin to assist with the removal of the cooked cake.

Sift the flour, almond meal, baking powder and cinnamon into a large bowl. Set aside.

Drain the pineapple – you can save the juice for another purpose. Add the pineapple, banana, apple, passionfruit pulp, eggs and butter and stir until combined. Spread the mixture into the prepared tin and sprinkle over the coconut. Bake for 28–33 minutes or until a skewer inserted into the centre comes out clean.

Remove from the oven and leave to cool for 10 minutes before gently transferring to a wire rack to cool completely.

The cake will keep in an airtight container for 2–3 days.

*This is a great way to use up bananas that are past their best. I like to slice this loaf, pop small squares of baking paper between the slices to stop them sticking together and freeze them in a sealed container. My eldest son is a particular fan of this cake. He loves it for school lunches.*

# Seeded banana & pear loaf

### SERVES 10–12

170 g (½ cup) rice malt syrup
125 g (½ cup) natural yoghurt
2 eggs
50 g (1¾ oz) butter, melted
3 teaspoons natural vanilla extract
2 overripe bananas, mashed
1 pear (about 230 g/8 oz), unpeeled
    and grated
300 g (10½ oz) Gluten-free flour
    blend #2 (see page 145)
3 teaspoons baking powder
2 teaspoons monk fruit extract
    powder (optional)
½ teaspoon bicarbonate of soda
    (baking soda)
1 tablespoon sunflower seeds
1 tablespoon pumpkin seeds
extra butter, to serve (optional)

Preheat the oven to 160°C/320°F (fan-forced). Grease an 11.5 cm × 21.5 cm (4½ in × 8½ in) loaf (bar) tin and line the base and two long sides with a piece of non-stick baking paper, extending the paper about 4 cm (1½ in) above the sides of the tin to assist with the removal of the cooked loaf.

Whisk the rice malt syrup, yoghurt, eggs, butter and vanilla extract together in a large mixing bowl. Stir in the banana and pear. Sift in the flour, baking powder, monk fruit extract powder (if using) and bicarbonate of soda and stir until combined.

Spoon the mixture into the prepared tin, smooth the surface and sprinkle with the seeds. Bake for 60–65 minutes or until a skewer inserted into the centre comes out clean. Remove from the oven and cool for 5 minutes before transferring to a wire rack to cool completely. Serve with extra butter if you like.

The cake will keep in an airtight container for 2–3 days.

*You will need at least five mandarins for this recipe – make sure you keep two of them whole, for slicing. This cake is beautifully moist with slightly savoury, grassy notes from the olive oil and bay leaves, and freshness from the mandarin. If mandarins are out of season, this cake works perfectly well with oranges, blood oranges or Meyer lemons.*

# Mandarin & bay leaf olive oil loaf

## SERVES 10

160 ml (⅔ cup) mild extra-virgin
   olive oil
4 fresh bay leaves, crumpled/
   bruised, plus extra to decorate
   (optional)
5–6 mandarins (about 600 g/
   1 lb 5 oz), depending on their size
100 g (⅓ cup) Apple purée
   (see page 148)
3 eggs
225 g (8 oz) Gluten-free flour
   blend #2 (see page 145)
2 teaspoons baking powder
2 teaspoons monk fruit extract
   powder
¼ teaspoon bicarbonate of soda
   (baking soda)
¼ teaspoon salt

Heat the olive oil and bay leaves in a small saucepan over low heat for about 10 minutes or until bubbles start to form around the leaves. Set aside to cool and infuse, about 30 minutes. Remove and discard the bay leaves, reserving the oil.

Finely zest and juice 3 or 4 mandarins – you need 2 teaspoons of zest and 80 ml (⅓ cup) of juice. Thinly slice the remaining whole unpeeled mandarins. Set aside.

Preheat the oven to 160°C/320°F (fan-forced). Grease an 11.5 cm × 21.5 cm (4¼ in × 8¼ in) loaf (bar) tin and line the base and two long sides with a piece of non-stick baking paper, extending the paper about 4 cm (1½ in) above the sides of the tin to assist with the removal of the cooked loaf.

Whisk the cooled infused olive oil, apple purée, mandarin zest and juice and eggs together in a large mixing bowl. Sift in the flour, baking powder, monk fruit extract powder, bicarbonate of soda and salt and stir until combined. Spread into the prepared tin and top with the mandarin slices, slightly overlapping them along the centre, as they will spread out as the cake rises. Decorate with the extra bay leaves, if using.

Bake for 50–55 minutes or until a skewer inserted into the centre comes out clean. Remove from the oven and leave to cool for 5 minutes before transferring to a wire rack to cool completely.

The cake will keep in an airtight container for 2–3 days.

*The nuttiness and extra flavour that comes from browned butter is fantastic. Just don't walk away from the pan as those delicious milk solids will change from toasty-brown to nearly burnt in the blink of an eye.*

# Brown butter loaf with brown butter frosting

## SERVES 10

125 g (4½ oz) butter
170 g (½ cup) rice malt syrup
small handful of hazelnuts
150 g (5¼ oz) Gluten-free flour
   blend #2 (see page 145)
90 g (¾ cup) almond meal
2 teaspoons baking powder
2 teaspoons monk fruit extract
   powder
3 eggs
1 tablespoon natural vanilla extract
pinch of salt

### BROWN BUTTER FROSTING

100 g (3½ oz) butter
100 g (3½ oz) cream cheese,
   softened
2 tablespoons rice malt syrup
1 teaspoon natural vanilla extract
pinch of salt

Preheat the oven to 160°C/320°F (fan-forced). Line a baking tray with non-stick baking paper. Grease an 11.5 cm × 21.5 cm (4¼ in × 8¼ in) loaf (bar) tin and line the base and two long sides with a piece of non-stick baking paper, extending the paper about 4 cm (1½ in) above the sides of the tin to assist with the removal of the cooked loaf.

Heat the butter in a small saucepan over low heat until melted and the milk solids (the little specks that separate from the liquid portion of the butter) become golden brown and give off a delicious nutty aroma. Swirl the pan so you can see the colour of the solids through the foam. Remove from the heat immediately and dunk the base of the pan in a sink of cold water to stop the cooking process. Whisk in the rice malt syrup and set the pan aside for the mixture to cool to room temperature – it should still be liquid.

Spread the hazelnuts over the prepared baking tray and bake for 5–8 minutes or until fragrant and the skins have loosened. Let the nuts cool slightly then rub them in a clean tea towel to remove the loose skins. Discard the skins and roughly chop the nuts.

Sift the flour, almond meal, baking powder and monk fruit extract powder into a large bowl. Set aside.

Beat the eggs and vanilla extract with an electric mixer until frothy. Add the salt, then continue to beat until the mixture is very thick and creamy – the mixture should leave a ribbon trail across the surface. Depending on your mixer, this could take up to 10 minutes. While still beating, gradually add the butter mixture.

Gently fold in the sifted flour mixture in two batches. Pour into the prepared tin and bake for 35–40 minutes or until a skewer inserted into the centre comes out clean. Remove from the oven and leave to cool for 5 minutes before transferring to a wire rack to cool completely.

For the brown butter frosting, brown the butter as directed above. Pour into a small bowl and refrigerate until set. Beat the solidified butter with an electric mixer until pale and creamy. Add the cream cheese, rice malt syrup, vanilla extract and salt and beat until smooth and fluffy. Spread the cooled cake with the frosting and sprinkle over the hazelnuts.

The cake will keep in an airtight container for 2–3 days.

# FOUR

# Celebration Cakes

*Roasted strawberries are really delicious. I especially love them with orange juice and rosewater.*

# Hazelnut sponge with roasted strawberries & ricotta

SERVES 8–10

4 eggs
115 g (⅓ cup) rice malt syrup
110 g (4 oz) Gluten-free flour blend #2 (see page 145)
110 g (1 cup) hazelnut meal
2 teaspoons baking powder
1 tablespoon finely grated orange zest
100 g (3½ oz) butter, melted
3 teaspoons rosewater
rose petals, to decorate (optional)

## ROASTED STRAWBERRIES AND WHIPPED RICOTTA

500 g (1 lb 2 oz) strawberries, hulled and halved if large
juice of 1 orange
2 teaspoons rosewater, plus extra to taste
500 g (1 lb 2 oz) fresh firm ricotta
¼ teaspoon monk fruit extract powder, to taste (optional)

Preheat the oven to 150°C/300°F (fan-forced). Very lightly grease a deep 20 cm (8 in) cake tin and line the base with non-stick baking paper.

Beat the eggs and rice malt syrup in a large bowl with an electric mixer until thick and creamy, and the mixture leaves a thick trail when the beaters are lifted. Depending on your mixer, this may take about 10 minutes.

Sift the flour, hazelnut meal and baking powder into a large bowl, returning any coarse hazelnut meal to the bowl with the flour. Gently fold the flour mixture into the egg mixture in two batches. Add the orange zest, melted butter and rosewater and gently fold through the mixture until just combined. Pour the mixture into the prepared tin, gently smooth the surface with a spatula and bake for 25–30 minutes, or until springy to touch in the centre and just starting to pull away from the side of the tin.

Remove from the oven and leave to cool for 15 minutes. Loosen the cake from the side of the tin before turning out onto a wire rack to cool completely.

For the roasted strawberries and whipped ricotta, put the strawberries, orange juice and rosewater in a shallow roasting tin, cover loosely with foil and roast for 25–30 minutes, or until the strawberries are just starting to collapse. Remove from the oven and set aside to cool.

Whiz the ricotta in a food processor until smooth and silky. Add 8–10 of the roasted strawberries and about 1 tablespoon of the syrup from the roasting tin. Whiz to combine, then taste the mixture and add a little more fruit, syrup, rosewater or monk fruit extract powder to get a balanced flavour and a smooth, spreadable consistency. Cover and refrigerate until required.

Slice the cooled cake in half horizontally using a long sharp serrated knife. Place the bottom layer on a serving plate or cake stand and spread over about half of the whipped ricotta mixture. Top with the remaining cake, whipped ricotta, roasted strawberries and a drizzle of the syrup. Decorate with rose petals for extra prettiness, if desired.

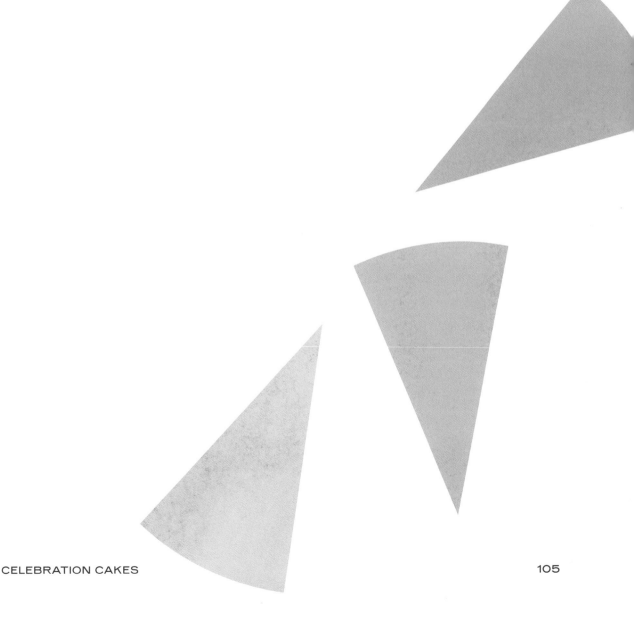

Hazelnut sponge with roasted strawberries & ricotta

**Carrot cake with lemon cream cheese frosting**

*It's hard to beat a great carrot cake with lemony cream cheese frosting.*
*The 'naked' method used here is quick and easy, with spectacular results.*
*Decorate the cake with edible flowers from the garden, if you have them.*

# Carrot cake with lemon cream cheese frosting

## SERVES 16–20

160 g (1 cup) dextrose

310 ml (1¼ cups) macadamia or
    sunflower oil

200 g (⅔ cup) Apple purée
    (see page 148)

6 eggs

3 carrots (about 350 g /12½ oz),
    finely grated

150 g (1½ cups) walnuts or pecans,
    roughly chopped (optional)

300 g (10½ oz) Gluten-free flour
    blend #2 (see page 145)

100 g (3½ oz) almond meal

3 teaspoons baking powder

1 tablespoon ground cinnamon

1 teaspoon ground nutmeg

½ teaspoon ground cloves

1 × quantity Lemon cream
    cheese frosting (see page 150)

edible flowers, to decorate
    (optional)

Preheat the oven to 160°C/320°F (fan-forced). Grease three 20 cm (8 in) round cake tins and line the bases with non-stick baking paper. If you don't have three tins, you can cook the cakes in two batches.

Whisk the dextrose, oil, apple purée and eggs together in a large bowl until well combined. Stir in the carrot and nuts (if using), then sift in the flour, almond meal, baking powder and spices, and stir until well combined.

Divide the cake batter evenly among the prepared tins (I like to weigh each tin to make sure they are roughly the same). Smooth the surface with a spatula and bake for 20–25 minutes until a skewer inserted into the centre comes out clean. Remove from the oven and leave to cool for 10 minutes before turning out onto a wire rack to cool completely.

Make the lemon cream cheese frosting.

If the cakes are slightly domed, trim the tops off to level them with a long sharp serrated knife.

Put a little dollop of the frosting in the centre of a serving plate and place four strips of baking paper around the edge. This will help to keep the plate clean of any icing. Place one layer of cake on the prepared plate. Spread about 160 g (1 cup) of the frosting over the cake, taking it just over the edge. Repeat with the remaining layers, placing the top layer of the cake bottom-side up (to achieve a sharp edge). Spread the remaining frosting over the top and side of the cake. Smooth off any excess frosting to achieve a 'naked' effect, just exposing the side of the cake. Remove the protective strips of baking paper from under the edge of the cake. Decorate with edible flowers, if desired.

The cake can be made a day in advance and stored in the fridge, covered loosely with plastic wrap. Decorate with flowers, just before serving.

*This show-stopper can be prepared a day in advance, although you may need to remove a shelf from your fridge to make enough room! Bake the cake, layer, frost and drizzle it with chocolate, then chill until about one hour before serving for the frosting to come back to room temperature. You can make the peanut brittle in advance (just make sure you store it in an airtight container), but don't add it to the cake until ready to serve.*

# Chocolate layer cake with peanut butter frosting

## SERVES 20–24

2 × quantities Everyday chocolate
   cake (see page 89), omitting
   the icing
1 × quantity Peanut butter frosting
   (see page 151)
2 tablespoons roasted black
   sesame seeds
handful of freshly popped popcorn

### PEANUT BRITTLE

240 g (1¼ cups) dextrose
1 tablespoon glucose syrup
75 g (2¾ oz) butter, chopped
¼ teaspoon bicarbonate of soda
   (baking soda)
150 g (1 cup) roasted salted peanuts

### CHOCOLATE DRIZZLE

100 g (3¼ oz) dark chocolate
   (70–85% cocoa solids),
   roughly chopped
100 g (3¼ oz) butter, chopped
2 teaspoons glucose syrup

Make the chocolate cakes, omitting the icing. You will need four layers of cake for this recipe.

To make the peanut brittle, line two large baking trays with non-stick baking paper. Put the dextrose, glucose syrup and 80 ml (⅓ cup) of water in a large saucepan over medium–high heat. Cook, gently swirling occasionally, until the glucose has dissolved. Bring to the boil and cook, without stirring, until you have a golden caramel, about 10 minutes. Remove from the heat and add the butter gradually, whisking well between each addition, until combined. Stir in the bicarbonate of soda, taking care as the mixture will bubble up slightly. Working quickly, stir in the peanuts and pour the mixture over one of the prepared trays. Place another piece of baking paper on top and use a rolling pin to flatten the mixture as much as possible. When the caramel is cool enough to handle – about 5 minutes – stretch sections of the mixture, starting from the edges, to create interesting shapes. Set aside to cool. Snap larger sections into shards. Any leftovers can be stored in an airtight container for up to 1 week.

Make the peanut butter frosting.

Put a little dollop of frosting in the centre of a serving plate and place four strips of baking paper around the edge. This will help to keep the plate clean of any icing. Place one layer of cake on the prepared plate. Spread about 80 g (¼ cup) of the peanut butter frosting over the cake, taking it just over the edge. Repeat with the remaining three layers, placing the top layer of the cake bottom-side up (to achieve a sharp edge). Spread a little more frosting thinly over the top and side of the cake. Scrape off any excess frosting and discard it (especially if it contains crumbs). This first layer is called the 'crumb coat' and will keep the final layer of icing crumb-free. Put the cake in the fridge for the frosting to firm up, about 30 minutes.

For the final layer of icing, spread the top and side of the cake generously with the remaining frosting, smoothing the side with a long spatula. Using a gentle throwing action, throw pinches of the sesame seeds at the base of the cake. Most of it should stick! Put the cake back in the fridge for the icing to firm, about 30 minutes.

To make the chocolate drizzle, combine the chocolate, butter and glucose syrup in a heatproof bowl and melt over a saucepan of simmering water. Stir until combined. Remove from the heat and set aside to cool to almost room temperature. The mixture needs to be runny enough to pour, but not so warm that it will melt the frosting on the cake. Working quickly, pour the chocolate onto the top of the cake and use an offset spatula to spread it evenly over the top, allowing the mixture to drip down the side. Remove the protective strips of baking paper from under the edge of the cake. Just before serving, decorate the top of the cake with the shards of the peanut brittle and the popcorn.

The undecorated cake can be made a day in advance and stored in the fridge. Once decorated, it is best eaten straight away. The cake is best served at room temperature; otherwise the frosting will be very firm.

**Chocolate layer cake with peanut butter frosting**

Coconut matcha
cake with matcha
cake pops

*Matcha green tea powder has a great flavour and colour. The cake pops add an additional fun element.*

# Coconut matcha cake with matcha cake pops

## SERVES 16–20

2 × quantities Coconut cake (see page 90), omitting the syrup
1 tablespoon matcha green tea powder
roasted black sesame seeds, to decorate

### MATCHA CAKE POPS

350 g (12¼ oz) coconut cake trimmings
100 g (3½ oz) cream cheese, softened
40 g (1½ oz) butter, softened
1 tablespoon rice malt syrup
¼ teaspoon matcha green tea powder
200 g (7 oz) dark chocolate (70–85% cocoa solids), roughly chopped
1 tablespoon melted virgin coconut oil
15–20 lollipop sticks
2 tablespoons roasted black sesame seeds

Make the coconut cakes, adding 2 teaspoons of matcha to the flour mixture for each cake. Cool completely and trim the top of each cake with a long sharp serrated knife. Set aside the trimmings for the cake pops. You will need about 350 g (12¼ oz) of trimmings in total to make the cake pops.

For the cake pops, crumble the cake trimmings with your fingertips to resemble breadcrumbs. Beat the cream cheese, butter, rice malt syrup and matcha in a large bowl with an electric mixer until light and fluffy. Add the cake crumbs and stir until well combined. Roll tablespoonfuls of the mixture into balls and refrigerate for 1–2 hours or until firm.

Combine the chocolate and coconut oil in a heatproof bowl and melt over a saucepan of simmering water. Stir to combine, then remove from the heat and leave to cool slightly.

Remove the cake pop balls from the fridge and insert a lollipop stick into each ball. Dip about half the cake balls fully in the chocolate to coat, allowing the excess chocolate to drip off, then sprinkle immediately with sesame seeds. Insert each cake pop stick into a foam block or place on a baking tray lined with baking paper. Refrigerate until set. For variation, half-dip some of the pops in the chocolate and leave some naked.

## COCONUT SWISS MERINGUE BUTTERCREAM

½ × quantity Swiss meringue buttercream (see page 152), omitting the natural vanilla extract
2 tablespoons coconut cream
a few drops of natural coconut extract (optional)

Make the Swiss meringue buttercream, omitting the vanilla extract. Add the coconut cream and coconut extract (if using) gradually, beating with an electric mixer on low speed until combined.

Put a little dollop of the frosting in the centre of a serving plate and place four strips of baking paper around the edge. This will help to keep the plate clean of any icing. Place one of the cakes on the prepared plate. Spread about 160 g (1 cup) of the buttercream over the cake, taking it just over the edge. Top with the second cake, placing it bottom-side up (to achieve a sharp edge). Spread the remaining buttercream over the top and side of the cake. Remove the protective strips of baking paper from under the edge of the cake and add the cake pops to the top of the cake. Decorate with a sprinkling of black sesame seeds and serve.

The cake can be made a day in advance and stored in the fridge, but is best served at room temperature or only slightly chilled. Cover carefully with plastic wrap once the buttercream has set.

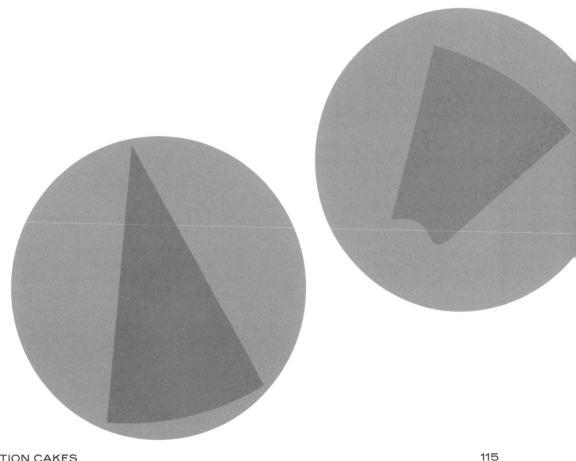

*This banana cream cheese frosting is sublime! The pineapple flowers take some time to dry out, but they don't require much effort. I've found that I get the best results with a ripe pineapple – the flowers have a better, brighter colour and dehydrate more rapidly. They're not only pretty, but also edible and truly delicious. The pineapple flowers can be made a few days in advance.*

# Hummingbird layer cake with pineapple flowers

## SERVES 16–20

1 ripe pineapple
2 × quantities Hummingbird cake
   (see page 95), omitting the flaked
   coconut topping
citrus leaves, to decorate

### BANANA CREAM CHEESE FROSTING

1 small banana, peeled
2 × quantities Lemon cream cheese
   frosting (see page 150), keeping
   the lemon juice separate

Preheat the oven to 80°C/175°F (fan-forced). Line two large baking trays with non-stick baking paper.

Top and tail the pineapple and cut away the skin. There will be some pineapple 'eyes' remaining, but don't worry, you can trim them later. Cut the pineapple into discs with a very sharp knife, about 2 mm (⅛ in) thick. Trim any remaining 'eyes', if necessary, and blot the pineapple discs on paper towel to soak up the excess moisture.

Place the pineapple discs on the prepared trays in a single layer and bake for 2–2¼ hours, turning every 30 minutes, until the discs are almost dry and the edges are starting to curl up. Lightly press the discs into mini-muffin or cupcake tins to create flower-like shapes. Bake for a further 30 minutes or until the flowers hold their shapes when lifted. Leave to cool in the tins. If not using straight away, store in an airtight container for 3–4 days.

Cut one-third off the length of each hummingbird cake. You will end up with two 20 cm (8 in) (approximately) squares and two rectangles to create three layers.

To make the banana cream cheese frosting, mash the banana in a bowl with a fork until quite smooth. You will need about 95 g (3¼ oz) of mashed banana. Stir in the lemon juice from the lemon cream cheese frosting and set aside.

Make the lemon cream cheese frosting, then beat in the banana mixture at the same time as the dextrose. Spoon about 160 g (1 cup) of the frosting into a piping bag with a 1.5 cm (½ in) plain nozzle. Refrigerate until required.

Put a little dollop of frosting in the centre of a serving plate and place four strips of baking paper around the edge. This will help to keep the plate clean of any icing. Place one of the square cakes on the prepared plate. Spread about 160 g (5¼ oz) of the frosting over the cake, taking it just over the edges. Repeat with the two rectangles, then the final square of cake, which you should place bottom-side up (to achieve sharp edges). Spread the remaining frosting over the top and sides of the cake. Remove the protective strips of baking paper from under the edges of the cake. Pipe little dollops of reserved frosting on the cake and decorate with the pineapple flowers and citrus leaves.

The cake can be stored in the fridge for up to 2 days, but is best served at room temperature or only slightly chilled.

# Hummingbird layer cake with pineapple flowers

Rainbow cake

*This spectacular cake is coloured with homemade natural food colouring. Its innocent exterior belies the fun rainbow layers hidden inside.*

# Rainbow cake

## SERVES 16–20

525 g (1 lb 3 oz) Gluten-free flour blend #2 (see page 145)
150 g (5½ oz) almond meal
2 tablespoons baking powder
3 teaspoons monk fruit extract powder
½ teaspoon bicarbonate of soda (baking soda)
375 g (13 oz) butter, softened
170 g (½ cup) rice malt syrup
6 eggs
225 g (¾ cup) Apple purée (see page 148)
2 tablespoons natural vanilla extract
180 ml (¾ cup) buttermilk
60 g (2 oz) shredded coconut
1 × quantity Swiss meringue buttercream (see page 152)

### NATURAL FOOD COLOURS

80 g (2 cups) baby spinach
1 beetroot (beet) (about 175 g/6 oz), peeled and roughly chopped
75 g (½ cup) frozen blackberries, thawed
1 carrot (about 120 g/4¼ oz), peeled and chopped

For the natural food colours, blend (I use a hand-held blender) the vegetables and fruit individually until puréed. Strain through a piece of muslin (cheesecloth), squeezing out as much juice as possible. You will need about 1 tablespoon of spinach juice, 2 tablespoons of beetroot juice for two pink cakes (one darker than the other), 5 teaspoons of blackberry juice and 2¼ tablespoons of carrot juice, plus about 2 teaspoons of each juice per 2 tablespoons of shredded coconut.

Preheat the oven to 160°C/320°F (fan-forced). Grease five 20 cm (8 in) round cake tins and line the bases with non-stick baking paper. If you don't have five tins, you can cook the cakes in batches.

Sift the flour, almond meal, baking powder, monk fruit extract powder and bicarbonate of soda into a large bowl and whisk to combine. Beat the butter and rice malt syrup with an electric mixer until light and fluffy. Gradually add the eggs, beating well between each addition and adding a tablespoon or two of the flour mixture, if it seems like the batter is splitting. Beat in the apple purée and vanilla extract. Fold in the remaining dry ingredients alternately with the buttermilk.

Divide the cake batter evenly between five separate bowls (I weigh it – about 400 g/14 oz per cake). Stir a different colouring into each bowl, adding a little more colouring if you would like a darker shade. Spoon into the prepared tins, smooth the surface with a spatula and bake for 15–18 minutes, or until a skewer inserted into the centre comes out clean. Remove from the oven and leave to cool for 5 minutes before turning out onto wire racks to cool.

Turn the oven down to 50°C/120°F (fan-forced). Divide 2 tablespoons of the shredded coconut among five small bowls and stir about 2 teaspoons of colouring into each bowl. Keeping the colours separate, spread the coconut on baking trays lined with baking paper and bake for 20–30 minutes, stirring often, until completely dry. Set aside to cool.

Make the Swiss meringue buttercream. If the cakes are slightly domed, trim the tops off to level them with a long sharp serrated knife.

Put a little dollop of buttercream in the centre of a serving plate and place four strips of baking paper around the edge. This will help to keep the plate clean of any icing. Place one layer of cake on the prepared plate. Spread about 120 g (¾ cup) of the buttercream over the top, taking it just over the edge. Repeat with the remaining layers, placing the top layer bottom-side up (to achieve a sharp edge). Spread more buttercream thinly over the top and side of the cake. Scrape off any excess buttercream and discard it. This first later is called the 'crumb coat' and will help to keep your final layer of icing crumb-free. Put the cake in the fridge for the icing to firm up, about 30 minutes.

For the final layer of icing, spread the top and side of the cake generously with the remaining buttercream. Sprinkle with the coloured shredded coconut to decorate. The cake can be stored in the fridge for several hours before serving, but it is best served at room temperature; otherwise the buttercream icing will be very firm.

# FIVE

# Sweet Endings

*If you have a tree overflowing with lemons, this recipe is a great way to use them up. You will need about four lemons for this recipe. I love the tartness and the silky texture of this lemony tart, and the crust is a versatile gluten-free beauty.*

# Lemon tart

## SERVES 10–12

1 tablespoon finely grated
   lemon zest
160 ml (¾ cup) freshly squeezed
   lemon juice
85 g (¼ cup) rice malt syrup
180 g (¾ cup) mascarpone
4 eggs, plus 1 egg extra, lightly
   beaten, for brushing
cream, crème fraîche or creamy
   yoghurt, to serve (optional)

### ALMOND PASTRY CRUST

240 g (2 cups) almond meal
2 tablespoons coconut flour
½ teaspoon monk fruit extract
   powder (optional)
60 g (2 oz) virgin coconut oil, chilled
   to solidify then roughly chopped
1 egg
2–4 teaspoons iced water

Preheat the oven to 160°C/320°F (fan-forced).

For the almond pastry crust, place the almond meal, coconut flour, monk fruit extract powder (if using) and solid coconut oil in a food processor and pulse until the coconut oil is mixed evenly throughout the mixture – you will still see small flecks of the solid coconut oil. Add the egg and, with the processor running, add enough water for the mixture to form coarse crumbs. It should cling together when pressed between your fingertips. Distribute the crumbs evenly over the base and up the side of a fluted 23 cm × 3 cm (9 in × 1¼ in) round loose-based tart tin, then press the mixture firmly into the base and side of the tin with your fingertips.

Cover the crust with a sheet of non-stick baking paper and fill with baking weights, or dry rice or beans. Blind bake for 10 minutes, then remove from the oven and take out the weights and paper. Brush the crust with the extra beaten egg and bake for a further 10 minutes or until the crust is cooked through and the sides are lightly coloured. Remove from the oven and set aside to cool.

Whisk the lemon zest and juice and rice malt syrup in a bowl until the syrup dissolves. Add the mascarpone and eggs and whisk gently until combined. Try not to whisk too vigorously or you will end up with little bubbles sitting on top of the cooked tart.

Put the cooled crust on a baking tray and place on the oven shelf. Pour the lemon mixture carefully into the crust. Bake for 25–30 minutes or until set with a slight wobble in the centre. Remove from the oven and cool in the tin. Serve at room temperature or chilled with cream, crème fraîche or yoghurt, if desired.

*This tart is perfect for when you need something light and lovely to finish a meal. Prepare the labne the night before for a luscious, thick texture. Make sure you buy pot-set yoghurt, rather than stirred or creamy yoghurt – it will strain more easily.*

# Creamy raspberry & orange tart

**SERVES 6**

120 g (½ cup) mascarpone
about 1½ tablespoons orange liqueur
    or freshly squeezed orange juice
125 g (4½ oz) fresh raspberries
rice malt syrup, to serve (optional)

### LABNE

250 g (1 cup) natural pot-set yoghurt
1 teaspoon finely grated orange zest

### ALMOND PASTRY CRUST

120 g (1 cup) almond meal
1 tablespoon coconut flour
¼ teaspoon monk fruit extract
    powder (optional)
30 g (1 oz) virgin coconut oil, chilled
    to solidify and roughly chopped
1 egg white

To make the labne, combine the yoghurt and orange zest and place in a sieve lined with muslin (cheesecloth). Place over a bowl, then cover and pop in the fridge for 12–24 hours to drain and thicken. This makes a little more labne than is needed for this recipe – save any leftovers to dollop on your breakfast cereal.

Preheat the oven to 160°C/320°F (fan-forced).

For the almond pastry crust, whiz the almond meal, coconut flour, monk fruit extract powder (if using) and solid coconut oil in a food processor until the coconut oil is mixed evenly throughout the mixture – you will still see small flecks of the solid coconut oil. Add the egg white and pulse until the mixture forms coarse crumbs. It should cling together when pressed between your fingertips.

Distribute the crumbs evenly over the base and up the side of a fluted 20 cm × 3 cm (8 in × 1¼ in) round loose-based tart tin, then press the mixture firmly into the base and side of the tin with your fingertips. The layer will seem very thin, but don't worry, it will hold together very well.

Cover the crust with a sheet of non-stick baking paper and fill with baking weights, or dry rice or beans. Blind bake for 10 minutes, then remove the weights and paper and bake for a further 10 minutes or until the crust is cooked through and the sides are lightly coloured. Remove from the oven and set aside to cool.

Mix 130 g (½ cup) of the labne with the mascarpone and 1 tablespoon of the liqueur or orange juice until combined. Taste and add a little more liqueur or juice to adjust the flavour and consistency to your liking. Spread into the cooled crust.

Toss the raspberries with the remaining liqueur or orange juice and scatter over the top of the tart. Drizzle with a little rice malt syrup, if desired, and serve.

*You could use only apples for this recipe, but why not mix it up? Just about any apple or pear will work well for this dish. The Middle Eastern flavours are utterly delicious.*

# Orange blossom-baked apples & pears

## SERVES 6

3 large apples (about 600 g/
   1 lb 5 oz), cored

3 pears (about 600 g/1 lb 5 oz),
   cored

100 g (3½ oz) Medjool dates, pitted
   and roughly chopped

40 g (¼ cup) almonds, roughly
   chopped

35 g (¼ cup) roughly chopped
   dried apricots

finely grated zest and juice of
   2 oranges

1 tablespoon orange blossom water

30 g (1 oz) butter, softened

Labne (see page 126), creamy
   yoghurt or mascarpone, to serve

Preheat the oven to 160°C/320°F (fan-forced).

Use a small sharp knife to score a spiral around each piece of fresh fruit, cutting just through the skin.

Combine the dates, almonds, apricots, orange zest and 2 teaspoons of the orange blossom water in a bowl. Divide between the cored fruit, pushing it firmly into the cavity, then transfer the fruit to a 1 litre (34 fl oz) baking dish. Sprinkle over the remaining orange blossom water and the orange juice, and scatter with dots of butter.

Cover the dish with foil and bake for 30 minutes or until the whole fruit is just soft. Remove the foil and bake for a further 15–20 minutes or until tender.

Serve with labne, yoghurt or mascarpone.

*Pandan extract is available from Asian grocery stores. The strength can vary among brands, so add it gradually. You can prepare the crèmes the day before serving – they need to be well chilled before you 'brûlée' the top. You will need a kitchen blowtorch for this task. Don't be tempted to add too much syrup to the top of each crème – it will take too long to caramelise.*

# Coconut & pandan crème brûlée

## SERVES 6

400 ml (13¼ oz) tin coconut milk
250 ml (1 cup) thickened (double/
   heavy) cream
½–1 teaspoon pandan extract
2 eggs, plus 4 egg yolks
2 tablespoons rice malt syrup,
   plus extra for drizzling
tropical fruit, to serve (optional)

Preheat the oven to 150°C/300°F (fan-forced). Fold a clean tea towel into the base of a large, deep baking dish and place six 125 ml (½ cup) capacity ramekins on top of the towel.

Heat the coconut milk, cream and pandan extract in a saucepan over medium–low heat. Cook, stirring occasionally, until the mixture almost comes to the boil, about 10 minutes.

Meanwhile, gently whisk the eggs, egg yolks and rice malt syrup in a large heatproof bowl until well combined. Gradually whisk in the coconut milk mixture, then strain into a large heatproof jug. Stand for 5 minutes and, using a large spoon, remove and discard any foam from the top of the mixture.

Divide the mixture evenly among the ramekins. Place the baking dish on the shelf of the oven and carefully add enough boiling water to come halfway up the sides of the ramekins, ensuring that the tea towel is completely submerged. (This is easier than trying to transport a dish full of water from the bench to the oven.) Bake for 20–25 minutes or until the custards are set with a slight wobble in the centre. Cool for 30 minutes, then refrigerate for at least 3 hours until firm.

Working with one ramekin at a time, drizzle about 1 teaspoon of rice malt syrup over the surface of each crème. Caramelise the syrup carefully with a kitchen blowtorch, swirling the syrup over the surface as you go. Set aside to cool and harden, then repeat with the remaining brûlées. Serve with tropical fruit, if desired.

*To make this aromatic pudding extra special, you can 'brûlée' the top. Just follow the instructions for the Coconut & pandan crème brûlée on page 130.*

# Baked makrut lime & coconut rice pudding

## SERVES 4–6

65 g (⅓ cup) medium-grain rice
4 makrut lime leaves, bruised, plus extra finely shredded to serve
1 stalk lemongrass, cut into sections, split and bruised
1 vanilla bean, split and seeds scraped
1 tablespoon rice malt syrup (optional)
600 ml (20½ fl oz) full-cream (whole) milk
400 ml (13½ fl oz) tin coconut milk
1 teaspoon monk fruit extract powder
lime segments, to serve

Preheat the oven to 160°C/320°F (fan-forced).

Combine the rice, bruised lime leaves, lemongrass, vanilla bean and seeds, rice malt syrup (if using) and the milks in a saucepan over medium heat. Cook, stirring occasionally, for 8–10 minutes or until the mixture just comes to a simmer. Remove from the heat and set aside for 20 minutes for the flavours to infuse.

Remove and discard the lime leaves, lemongrass and the vanilla bean. Stir in the monk fruit extract powder (if using) and pour the mixture into a 1 litre (34 fl oz) ovenproof dish (or four 250 ml/1 cup capacity ramekins). Bake, stirring occasionally, for 1 hour 15 minutes–1 hour 30 minutes for the large dish and 1 hour–1 hour 10 minutes for the ramekins, or until the rice is tender and the mixture is very creamy. When a skin begins to form, try to stir underneath the skin if you can. Stir less frequently towards the end of the cooking time.

Remove from the oven and set aside for 10 minutes to rest before serving. Sprinkle with shredded lime leaves and lime segments, and serve warm or cold.

NATURAL BAKES

*You can blanch and peel your fruit if you like, but I don't think it's necessary for this crumble. Try other stone fruit when in season – apricots, plums and cherries would all work very well.*

# Peach, nectarine & ginger crumble

## SERVES 6–8

3 peaches (about 600 g/1 lb 5 oz)
3 nectarines (about 600 g/1 lb 5 oz)
1 tablespoon cornflour (cornstarch)
1 teaspoon finely grated fresh ginger
finely grated zest and juice of
   1 orange
cream, crème fraîche or thick
   yoghurt, to serve

### CRUMBLE TOPPING

70 g (⅔ cup) quinoa flakes
60 g (½ cup) pecans, roughly
   chopped
25 g (½ cup) flaked coconut
10 g (⅓ cup) puffed wholegrain rice
1 teaspoon ground ginger
80 g (2¾ oz) butter or virgin
   coconut oil, melted
2 tablespoons rice malt syrup

Preheat the oven to 160°C/320°F (fan-forced).

Halve the peaches and nectarines, remove the stones and cut into wedges. Toss with the cornflour and ginger in a large bowl, and then with the orange zest and juice. Pile into a 1 litre (34 fl oz) baking dish or four 250 ml (1 cup) ramekins.

For the crumble topping, combine the quinoa flakes, pecans, coconut, puffed rice and ginger in a large bowl. Drizzle with the melted butter or oil and the rice malt syrup. Stir until well combined.

Sprinkle the crumble mixture over the fruit. Bake for 35–40 minutes or until the fruit is bubbling and the top is golden and crisp. Cover with foil if the top is browning too quickly. Serve with a dollop of cream, crème fraîche or thick yoghurt.

*The simple yet delicious filling for this pie is fabulous served with just a dollop of cream or yoghurt (even for breakfast) – yet the impressive lattice top takes it to the next level. It takes a bit of patience but is worth the effort. I don't bother with peeling the apples – you may as well get the extra fibre from the skin, I say.*

# Rhubarb & apple pie

### SERVES 6–8

1 × quantity Gluten-free rough puff pastry (see page 146)
gluten-free flour, for dusting
30 g (1 oz) butter
3 large apples (about 600 g/ 1 lb 5 oz), cored and thinly sliced
finely grated zest and juice of 1 orange
2 tablespoons rice malt syrup
450 g (1 lb) trimmed rhubarb, cut into 2.5 cm (1 in) pieces
2 tablespoons tapioca flour (tapioca starch) or cornflour (cornstarch)
1 teaspoon mixed spice (pumpkin pie spice)
1 egg, lightly beaten
cream, crème fraîche or creamy yoghurt, to serve

Roll out the pastry on a lightly floured surface to about 3 mm (⅛ in) thick. Cut a 1.5 cm (½ in) strip of pastry from the edge and press it around the rim of a 24 cm (9½ in) pie dish. Rub the rim of the dish with a little softened butter to help the pastry stick if necessary. This will create a nice finished edge on the pie when you add the lattice. Set aside in the fridge. Cut the remaining pastry into long strips 4 cm (1½ in) wide. You will need at least eight strips. Place on a baking paper–lined tray and refrigerate until required.

Melt the butter in a large saucepan over medium–low heat. Add the apple, orange zest and juice and rice malt syrup and cook for 3 minutes or until the apple is barely starting to soften. Add the rhubarb and cook for a further 2–3 minutes or until the rhubarb is lightly cooked but still holding its shape. Remove from the heat and stir in the tapioca flour or cornflour and mixed spice. Transfer to the pie dish and set aside to cool.

Preheat the oven to 190°C/375°F (fan-forced).

Brush the pastry on the rim of the pie dish with a little water and arrange the pastry strips in a lattice pattern over the filling, pressing the strips onto the pastry rim to seal and trimming any excess pastry. Brush lightly with the beaten egg, trying not to let it dribble down the sides of the pastry strips.

Bake for 20 minutes or until the pastry is starting to puff and is lightly coloured. Reduce the oven temperature to 160°C/320°F (fan-forced) and cook for another 15–20 minutes or until the pastry is golden and the filling is bubbling.

Remove from the oven and allow to settle for 10 minutes before serving with cream, crème fraîche or yoghurt.

*Tarte Tatin is a classic dessert and just as delicious made with rice malt syrup and gluten-free pastry. It really is a worthwhile exercise making your own pastry – rough puff is the cheat's version of puff, and so not quite as tricky to make. Don't throw your pastry scraps away: cut them into pieces, bake and enjoy the crunchy morsels later on. Make sure your apples are fresh and crisp from the new season for best results.*

# Tarte Tatin

## SERVES 8–10

6 granny smith apples (about 1 kg/2 lb 3 oz), peeled, cored and quartered
2 tablespoons freshly squeezed lemon juice
¼ teaspoon ground cinnamon
170 g (½ cup) rice malt syrup
40 g (1½ oz) butter, thinly sliced
½ × quantity Gluten-free rough puff pastry (see page 146)
gluten-free flour, for dusting
cream, crème fraîche or creamy yoghurt, to serve

Toss the apple with the lemon juice and cinnamon in a large bowl.

Drizzle the rice malt syrup over the base of a 20 cm (8 in) heavy-based ovenproof frying pan or tarte tatin pan and scatter with the butter. Add the apple quarters, cut-side up, tightly packing them in a single layer.

Cook the apple over medium heat for 10–15 minutes or until the syrup is beginning to caramelise and the apple is just tender. There will be quite a bit of juice in the pan. Remove from the heat and set aside to cool for about 30 minutes.

Meanwhile, preheat the oven to 190°C/375°F (fan-forced).

Roll out the pastry on a lightly floured surface to about 3 mm (¼ in) thick and cut a circle slightly larger than the pan. Prick the pastry all over with a fork and place it on top of the apple, easing the pastry edge down between the apple and the side of the pan.

Bake for 25–30 minutes or until the pastry is cooked through, puffed and a deep golden brown. You should see the juices bubbling up the sides. Remove from the oven and allow to settle for 10 minutes.

Place a large serving plate upside-down on top of the pan and carefully invert the tart onto the plate. Serve warm or cold with cream, crème fraîche or yoghurt.

*I love the combination of roasted rhubarb with the sweetness of strawberries. This dessert is finished off beautifully with the crispy topping. The crumble mixture even makes great biscuits if you roll it into balls, flatten slightly onto a tray and bake for about 15 minutes. Only add the rice malt syrup if you think the fruit is not at its peak, to balance out any tartness.*

# Rhubarb & strawberry crumble

## SERVES 6

450 g (1 lb) trimmed rhubarb, cut
    into 3 cm (1¼ in) pieces
500 g (1 lb 2 oz) strawberries,
    hulled and halved if large
2 teaspoons vanilla bean paste
1 tablespoon rice malt syrup
finely grated zest and juice of
    1 large orange
cream, crème fraîche or thick
    yoghurt, to serve

## CRISPY CRUMBLE TOPPING

100 g (3¼ oz) flaked coconut
50 g (1¾ oz) Gluten-free flour
    blend #1 (see page 144)
1 teaspoon ground cinnamon
80 g (2¾ oz) chilled butter, chopped
2 tablespoons rice malt syrup
40 g (½ cup) flaked almonds

Preheat the oven to 160°C/320°F (fan-forced).

In a large bowl, combine the rhubarb, strawberries, vanilla, rice malt syrup and the orange zest and juice. Pile the mixture into a 1.5 litre (51 fl oz) baking dish or six 250 ml (1 cup) ramekins.

For the crumble topping, combine the coconut, flour and cinnamon in a large bowl. Add the butter and drizzle with the rice malt syrup. Use your fingertips to rub in the butter and syrup until well combined. Stir in the almonds.

Sprinkle the crumble mixture over the top of the fruit, leaving little clumps of different sizes. Bake for 30–35 minutes or until the fruit is bubbling and the top is golden and crisp. Cover with foil if the top is browning too quickly. Serve with a dollop of cream, crème fraîche or thick yoghurt.

# Basics

*Fine brown rice flour, the protein flour in this blend, lends stability and structure to the crumb in cookies and biscuits, along with flavour, texture and body. It is softened by the potato starch that helps add lightness, and tapioca flour encourages a crust to form. The xanthan gum assists with the structure. For further information about gluten-free flours see page 8.*

# Gluten-free flour blend #1 (for biscuits and cookies)

**MAKES 550 G (1 LB 3 OZ)**

200 g (7 oz) fine brown rice flour
200 g (7 oz) potato starch
150 g (5¼ oz) tapioca flour
    (tapioca starch)
2 teaspoons xanthan gum

Sift the flours and xanthan gum together into a large bowl, then sift again (or whisk) to ensure the ingredients are evenly combined. Store in an airtight container, away from direct sunlight, for up to 3 months.

*Sorghum flour, the protein flour in this blend, lends stability and structure to the cake's crumb, along with flavour, texture and body. It is softened by the secondary starchy flours – potato and tapioca – that add lightness to cakes. The glutinous rice flour is great for texture, while the xanthan gum assists with the structure. For further information about gluten-free flours see page 8.*

# Gluten-free flour blend #2 (for cakes)

**MAKES 600 G (1 LB 5 OZ)**

300 g (10½ oz) sorghum flour
100 g (3½ oz) potato starch
100 g (3½ oz) tapioca flour (tapioca starch)
100 g (3½ oz) glutinous rice flour
2 teaspoons xanthan gum

Sift the flours and xanthan gum together into a large bowl, then sift again (or whisk) to ensure the ingredients are evenly combined. Store in an airtight container, away from direct sunlight, for up to 3 months.

*It's possible to make rough puff pastry with gluten-free flour, although it does require some patience! Keep a careful eye on the patches of butter, and ensure that they are always dusted with a little flour to prevent them bursting through your slowly developing dough. The slivers of butter that remain between the layers of dough give this pastry its flakiness and lift.*

# Gluten-free rough puff pastry

## MAKES 600 G (1 LB 5 OZ)

250 g (9 oz) Gluten-free flour pastry blend (see below), plus extra for dusting

¼ teaspoon salt

200 g (7 oz) cold butter, cut into 1 cm (½ in) pieces

80 ml (⅓ cup) iced water, plus extra if needed

80 ml (⅓ cup) cold full-cream (whole) milk

### GLUTEN-FREE FLOUR PASTRY BLEND (MAKES 300 G/10½ OZ)

150 g (5½ oz) sorghum flour

100 g (3½ oz) glutinous rice flour

25 g (1 oz) potato starch

25 g (1 oz) tapioca flour (tapioca starch)

1½ teaspoons xanthan gum

To make the gluten-free flour pastry blend, sift the flours and xanthan gum into a large bowl, then sift again (or whisk) to ensure the ingredients are evenly combined. You will need 250 g (9 oz) of flour for the rough puff pastry. There will be enough left over for dusting.

Mix the flour blend and salt together in a large bowl. Add the butter and toss through the flour with your fingertips until the butter is coated. Add the water and milk and mix to just combine, then press the mixture together to form a rough dough, taking care to leave the butter in lumps. Add a little more water if necessary, just to bring the dough together and to stop it cracking. Do not knead.

On a clean work surface lightly dusted with some of the remaining flour blend, press the pastry into a rectangle about 3 cm (1¼ in) thick. Roll it out to a 20 cm × 30 cm (8 in × 12 in) rectangle, ensuring that any patches of butter are dusted with a little more flour before they become exposed. It will seem very messy but don't worry, it will all come together. If you've made regular rough puff pastry before, you will note that this is a slower process with gluten-free flour.

Fold the dough into thirds, as you would to fold a letter, brushing off any excess flour as you go. Rotate the dough 90 degrees and then repeat the rolling and folding instructions, using extra flour to stop the dough sticking, and to lightly coat any bits of butter that stick out. It will still look quite rough at this stage with visible lumps of butter, but it should look more like a dough now.

Wrap the dough well in plastic wrap and chill for 30 minutes in the fridge. Repeat the above process twice more. The dough is ready to use after it has been chilled three times. The finished dough should be smooth and elastic, with fine slivers of butter between the layers of dough. If you cut through the dough with a sharp knife, you will see the layers quite clearly.

The dough will keep well-wrapped in plastic wrap in the fridge for 2–3 days. It can also be frozen for 3–4 weeks. Thaw in the fridge for several hours before use.

*This apple purée is used in a number of recipes in this book, particularly in the cakes chapters. It helps to add bulk to baked goods that have had the cane sugar removed, as well as providing natural sweetness and fibre.*

# Apple purée

MAKES 600 G (2 CUPS)

4 large apples (about 800 g/
     1 lb 12 oz)

Peel, core and roughly chop the apples. Place the apple and a splash of water in a saucepan over medium–low heat. Cover and cook, stirring occasionally, for 8–10 minutes, until the apple is tender. Stir and mash the apple, still over the heat, until broken down – it should be mushy and quite thick. Remove from the heat and set aside to cool.

It is fine to have a little texture in the apple sauce, but if you prefer a smooth purée, whiz the apple sauce in a food processor or use a hand-held blender to purée until smooth.

The apple purée will keep in an airtight container in the fridge for 3–4 days. It also freezes well for a couple of months – portion the sauce or purée into small containers or spoon into ice-cube trays, then freeze and seal in an airtight container.

*This fantastic jam is used in the Coconut raspberry jam slice on page 45 and the Jam duffins on page 66, but it is equally delicious spread on a slice of your favourite gluten-free bread. Make it with fresh berries when they are in season and plentiful, or use frozen berries any time of the year.*

# Raspberry chia jam

## MAKES 420 G (1½ CUPS)

500 g (1 lb 2 oz) fresh or frozen
    raspberries or mixed berries
2 tablespoons rice malt syrup
2 tablespoons freshly squeezed
    lemon juice
2 tablespoons chia seeds

Place the berries, rice malt syrup and lemon juice in a heavy-based saucepan over medium–low heat. Cook, stirring often, for about 30 minutes or until the berries are broken down and the mixture is slightly reduced and thickened. Remove from the heat and stir in the chia seeds. The mixture will thicken further as it cools.

Transfer the jam to a clean airtight container and store in the fridge for up to 2 weeks.

*This is a delicious and versatile frosting. Use the finest dextrose you can find (brands vary). If you think it may be a bit coarse, blend in a food processor (but don't lift the lid too quickly or you'll be covered in dextrose dust!), until you have an icing-sugar consistency.*

# Lemon cream cheese frosting

## MAKES 550 G (2½ CUPS)

250 g (1 cup) cream cheese, softened
finely grated zest of 1 lemon
125 g (4¼ oz) butter, chopped into cubes and softened
1 tablespoon freshly squeezed lemon juice
160 g (1 cup) dextrose

Beat the cream cheese and lemon zest with an electric mixer until smooth. Add the butter, 4–5 cubes at a time, and beat until light and fluffy. Add the lemon juice and then the dextrose, a few tablespoons at a time and beating well between each addition, until well combined.

Use straight away, or store in an airtight container in the fridge for 2–3 days. Before use, bring back to room temperature and re-beat until smooth and creamy.

*This deliciously moreish frosting can be used on cakes, cupcakes or as a filling for sandwiching biscuits and cookies.*

# Peanut butter frosting

**MAKES ABOUT 1 KG (5⅓ CUPS)**

375 g (13 oz) butter, softened
420 g (1½ cups) natural smooth peanut butter
120 g (¾ cup) dextrose
100 g (3½ oz) sour cream

Beat the butter and peanut butter in a large bowl with an electric mixer, until light and fluffy. Add the dextrose gradually, beating well between each addition. Add the sour cream and beat until combined. Refrigerate to keep cool if the room temperature is warm.

Use straight away, or store in an airtight container in the fridge for 2–3 days. Before use, bring back to room temperature and re-beat until smooth and creamy.

*This buttercream is so beautiful to work with. I like to use a small offset spatula to apply the icing – it makes the job so much easier. It is important that the butter is slightly softened as you beat it into the meringue mixture – it should be just soft enough for your fingertip to leave a dent in the butter when lightly pressed.*

# Swiss meringue buttercream

**MAKES 1.5 KG (3 LB 5 OZ)**

300 g (10¼ oz) egg white
   (from about 9 eggs)
520 g (3¼ cups) dextrose
700 g (1 lb 9 oz) butter, cut into
   cubes and slightly softened
   (it should be soft enough for your
   fingertip to leave a dent when
   the butter is lightly pressed)
1 tablespoon natural vanilla extract

Put the egg white and dextrose in a large heatproof bowl. Place the bowl over a saucepan of simmering water (the bowl shouldn't touch the water) and whisk until the dextrose dissolves and the egg white is warmed through. Test the mixture by rubbing a little between your thumb and forefinger – it should be smooth, not grainy. Remove from the heat.

Beat the egg white mixture with an electric mixer on medium-high speed until you have a thick and glossy meringue, and the side of the bowl is at room temperature when you touch it. This will take about 10 minutes, depending on your mixer.

Reduce the mixer speed to medium, then add the cubes of butter gradually, beating well between each addition, until the meringue is silky smooth. You may find that the mixture separates and curdles at some point in the mixing process – do not panic, if you keep beating it should come back together. If the room temperature is too warm (around 18°C/64°F is ideal) and the mixture seems quite soft, pop the bowl in the fridge for 10–15 minutes to cool it down. Add the vanilla extract and beat on low speed until combined.

Use the buttercream straight away or store in an airtight container in the fridge for up to 1 week. Before use, bring the buttercream back to room temperature and re-beat until smooth and creamy. Beat in a little more softened butter if the mixture starts to curdle, to bring it back together.

# Index

## A

**almond**
Almond, mandarin & orange blossom madeleines 52
Almond, rosewater & chocolate donut cakes 46
Almond mandarin cake 74
almond pastry crust 124, 126
Baked lemon cheesecake 80
Baked vanilla & pea donuts 60
Brown butter loaf with brown butter frosting 100–1
Carrot cake with lemon cream cheese frosting 108–9
Coconut raspberry jam slice 45
Cracked pepperberry shortbreads 26
Creamy raspberry & orange tart 126
crispy crumble topping 141
Fig, prune & cranberry crumble slice 57
frangipane 69
Hummingbird cake 95
Hummingbird layer cake with pineapple flowers 116–17
Jam duffins 66
Orange blossom–baked apples & pears 129
Pear & chocolate frangipane galettes 69
Rainbow cake 120–1
Rhubarb & strawberry crumble 141
Spiced apple & cream cheese muffins 64
Sweet potato, lime & poppy seed cake 92
Tahini shortbread buttons 18
Toasted almond, coconut & chia cookies 20

**apple**
Apple purée 148
Baked vanilla & pea donuts 60
Beetroot chocolate tray cake 54
Carrot, parsnip & cardamom loaf 77
Carrot cake with lemon cream cheese frosting 108–9
Chocolate layer cake with peanut butter frosting 110–11
Chocolaty sweet potato & macadamia cream cake 86–7
Coconut cake with citrus syrup 90
Coconut matcha cake with matcha cake pops 114–15
Everyday chocolate cake 89
Hummingbird cake 95
Hummingbird layer cake with pineapple flowers 116–17

Jam duffins 66
Mandarin & bay leaf olive oil loaf 98
Orange blossom–baked apples & pears 129
Rainbow cake 120–1
Rhubarb & apple pie 136
Spiced apple & cream cheese muffins 64
Spiced pumpkin donuts 58
Tarte Tatin 138
apricots: Orange blossom–baked apples & pears 129

**avocado**
avocado coconut icing 60
Baked vanilla & pea donuts 60

## B

Baked lemon cheesecake 80
Baked makrut lime & coconut rice pudding 132
Baked vanilla & pea donuts 60

**banana**
banana cashew cream 24
Banana chai blondies 42
banana cream cheese frosting 116–17
Chocolate sandwich cookies 24–5
Hummingbird cake 95
Hummingbird layer cake with pineapple flowers 116–17
Seeded banana & pear loaf 96
bay leaves: Mandarin & bay leaf olive oil loaf 98

**beans**
Almond, mandarin & orange blossom madeleines 52
Banana chai blondies 42
Chocolate, beetroot & orange cupcakes 48
Chocolate cake 72

**beetroot**
Beetroot chocolate tray cake 54
Chocolate, beetroot & orange cupcakes 48
natural food colours 120
Rainbow cake 120–1
berries see blackberries, blueberries, cranberries, raspberries, strawberries
biscotti, Rosemary, hazelnut & orange 37

**biscuits**
Gingernuts 30
Passionfruit cashew cream melting moments 32
Rosemary, hazelnut & orange biscotti 37
see also shortbread

**blackberry**
natural food colours 120
Rainbow cake 120–1
blondies, Banana chai 42
blueberry: Cookies & cream blueberry cheesecake 84
brittle, peanut 110
brown butter frosting 100
Brown butter loaf with brown butter frosting 100–1
Brown butter pecan shortbread fingers 23
Brownies with coconut–date swirl 40

**buttercream**
coconut swiss meringue buttercream 115
Swiss meringue buttercream 152

## C

cacao see chocolate
Cacao nib hazelnut cookies 12

**cakes**
Almond, rosewater & chocolate donut cakes 46
Beetroot chocolate tray cake 54
Brown butter loaf with brown butter frosting 100–1
Carrot, parsnip & cardamom loaf 77
Carrot cake with lemon cream cheese frosting 108–9
Chocolate cake 72
Chocolate layer cake with peanut butter frosting 110–11
Chocolaty sweet potato & macadamia cream cake 86–7
Coconut cake with citrus syrup 90
Coconut matcha cake with matcha cake pops 114–15
Everyday chocolate cake 89
Hazelnut sponge with roasted strawberries & ricotta 104–5
Hummingbird cake 95
Hummingbird layer cake with pineapple flowers 116–17
Mandarin & bay leaf olive oil loaf 98
matcha cake pops 114
Rainbow cake 120–1
Seeded banana & pear loaf 96
Sweet potato, lime & poppy seed cake 92
see also cheesecakes, cupcakes, loaves, slices

**cardamom**
Carrot, parsnip & cardamom loaf 77
Chai chia cupcakes 51

**carrot**
Carrot, parsnip & cardamom loaf 77

Carrot cake cookies 14
Carrot cake with lemon cream
    cheese frosting 108–9
natural food colours 120
Rainbow cake 120–1

**cashew**
Chocolate sandwich cookies 24–5
passionfruit cashew cream 32
Passionfruit cashew cream melting
    moments 32
Chai chia cupcakes 51

**cheese**
Creamy raspberry & orange tart 126
labne 126
see also cream cheese,
    mascarpone, ricotta

**cheesecake**
Baked lemon cheesecake 80
Cookies & cream blueberry
    cheesecake 84
Lime cheesecake tart 78
Peanut butter swirl cheesecake 83

**chia seed**
Chai chia cupcakes 51
Coconut raspberry jam slice 45
Jam duffins 66
Raspberry chia jam 149
Toasted almond, coconut & chia
    cookies 20
chickpea: Chai chia cupcakes 51

**chocolate**
Almond, rosewater & chocolate
    donut cakes 46
Banana chai blondies 42
Beetroot chocolate tray cake 54
Cacao nib hazelnut cookies 12
Chocolate, beetroot & orange
    cupcakes 48
Chocolate cake 72
chocolate drizzle 110–11
chocolate glaze 46
chocolate icing 89
Chocolate layer cake with peanut
    butter frosting 110–11
Chocolate sandwich cookies 24–5
Chocolaty sweet potato &
    macadamia cream cake 86–7
Coconut matcha cake with matcha
    cake pops 114–15
Cookies & cream blueberry
    cheesecake 84
Everyday chocolate cake 89
frangipane 69
Fudgy roasted cocoa cookies 34
matcha cake pops 114
Peanut butter cookies 17
Peanut butter swirl cheesecake 83
Pear & chocolate frangipane
    galettes 69

**cinnamon**
Banana chai blondies 42
Carrot, parsnip & cardamom loaf 77
Carrot cake with lemon cream
    cheese frosting 108–9
Chai chia cupcakes 51

cinnamon powder 68
crispy crumble topping 141
Hummingbird cake 95
Hummingbird layer cake with
    pineapple flowers 116–17
Jam duffins 66
Rhubarb & strawberry crumble 141
Spiced apple & cream cheese
    muffins 64
Tarte Tatin 138

**citrus**
citrus syrup 90
Coconut cake with citrus syrup 90
Coconut matcha cake with matcha
    cake pops 114–15
see also lemons, limes, mandarins,
    oranges
cloves: Carrot cake with lemon cream
    cheese frosting 108–9

**coconut**
almond pastry crust 124, 126
avocado coconut icing 60
Baked makrut lime & coconut rice
    pudding 132
Baked vanilla & pea donuts 60
Banana chai blondies 42
Brownies with coconut–date swirl
    40
Carrot cake cookies 14
Carrot, parsnip & cardamom loaf 77
Chocolaty sweet potato &
    macadamia cream cake 86–7
Coconut & pandan crème brûlée
    130
Coconut cake with citrus syrup 90
coconut–date swirl 40
Coconut matcha cake with matcha
    cake pops 114–15
Coconut raspberry jam slice 45
coconut swiss meringue
    buttercream 115
Creamy raspberry & orange tart 126
crispy crumble topping 141
crumble topping 135
Fig, prune & cranberry crumble
    slice 57
Hummingbird cake 95
Lemon tart 124
Lime cheesecake tart 78
macadamia vanilla cream 87
matcha cake pops 114
Peach, nectarine & ginger crumble
    135
Peanut butter swirl cheesecake 83
Rainbow cake 120–1
Rhubarb & strawberry crumble 141
Toasted almond, coconut & chia
    cookies 20

**coffee**
Chocolate layer cake with peanut
    butter frosting 110–11
Everyday chocolate cake 89

**cookies**
Cacao nib hazelnut cookies 12
Carrot cake cookies 14

Chocolate sandwich cookies 24–5
Fudgy roasted cocoa cookies 34
Peanut butter cookies 17
Toasted almond, coconut & chia
    cookies 20
Cookies & cream blueberry
    cheesecake 84
Cracked pepperberry shortbreads 26
cranberries: Fig, prune & cranberry
    crumble slice 57

**cream**
banana cashew cream 24
macadamia vanilla cream 87
passionfruit cashew cream 32
see also buttercream

**cream cheese**
Baked lemon cheesecake 80
banana cream cheese frosting
    116–17
brown butter frosting 100
Brown butter loaf with brown butter
    frosting 100–1
Carrot cake with lemon cream
    cheese frosting 108–9
Coconut matcha cake with matcha
    cake pops 114–15
Cookies & cream blueberry
    cheesecake 84
Hummingbird layer cake with
    pineapple flowers 116–17
Lemon cream cheese frosting 150
Lime cheesecake tart 78
matcha cake pops 114
Peanut butter swirl cheesecake 83
Spiced apple & cream cheese
    muffins 64
Creamy raspberry & orange tart 126
crème brûlée, Coconut & pandan 130
crispy crumble topping 141

**crumble**
Peach, nectarine & ginger crumble
    135
Rhubarb & strawberry crumble 141
crumble topping 135
Crunchy lemon myrtle & polenta
    shortbread 29

**cupcakes**
Chai chia cupcakes 51
Chocolate, beetroot & orange
    cupcakes 48

## D

**dates**
Baked lemon cheesecake 80
Brownies with coconut–date swirl
    40
Carrot, parsnip & cardamom loaf 77
Carrot cake cookies 14
coconut–date swirl 40
Orange blossom–baked apples &
    pears 129

**donut**
Almond, rosewater & chocolate
    donut cakes 46
Baked vanilla & pea donuts 60

Spiced pumpkin donuts 58
drizzle, chocolate 110–11
duffins, Jam 66

**E**

**eggs**
Coconut matcha cake with matcha cake pops 114–15
coconut swiss meringue buttercream 115
Rainbow cake 120–1
Swiss meringue buttercream 152
Everyday chocolate cake 89

**F**

fennel seeds: Pumpkin & fennel scones 83
Fig, prune & cranberry crumble slice 57
**flour**
Gluten-free flour blend #1 (for biscuits and cookies) 144
Gluten-free flour blend #2 (for cakes) 145
gluten-free flour pastry blend 146
food colour, natural 120
frangipane 69
**frosting**
banana cream cheese frosting 116–17
brown butter frosting 100
Lemon cream cheese frosting 150
Peanut butter frosting 151
*see also* icing
Fudgy roasted cocoa cookies 34

**G**

galettes, Pear & chocolate frangipane 69
**ginger**
Banana chai blondies 42
Carrot cake cookies 14
Chai chia cupcakes 51
crumble topping 135
Gingernuts 30
Lime cheesecake tart 78
Peach, nectarine & ginger crumble 135
Gingernuts 30
glaze, chocolate 46
Gluten-free flour blend #1 (for biscuits and cookies) 144
Gluten-free flour blend #2 (for cakes) 145
gluten-free flour pastry blend 146
Gluten-free rough puff pastry 146–7

**H**

**hazelnuts**
Brown butter loaf with brown butter frosting 100–1
Cacao nib hazelnut cookies 12
Cookies & cream blueberry cheesecake 84
Hazelnut sponge with roasted strawberries & ricotta 104–5
Rosemary, hazelnut & orange biscotti 37

Hummingbird cake 95
Hummingbird layer cake with pineapple flowers 116–17

**I**

**icing**
avocado coconut icing 60
chocolate icing 89
lime icing 51
orange and mascarpone topping 48
*see also* frosting

**J**

Jam duffins 66
jam, Raspberry chia 149

**L**

labne 126
**lemon**
Baked lemon cheesecake 80
banana cashew cream 24
banana cream cheese frosting 116–17
Carrot cake with lemon cream cheese frosting 108–9
Chocolate sandwich cookies 24–5
Crunchy lemon myrtle & polenta shortbread 29
Hummingbird layer cake with pineapple flowers 116–17
Lemon cream cheese frosting 150
Lemon tart 124
Pear & chocolate frangipane galettes 69
Raspberry chia jam 149
Tarte Tatin 138
lemon myrtle: Crunchy lemon myrtle & polenta shortbread 29
lemongrass: Baked makrut lime & coconut rice pudding 132
**lime**
avocado coconut icing 60
Baked vanilla & pea donuts 60
Chai chia cupcakes 51
Lime cheesecake tart 78
lime icing 51
Sweet potato, lime & poppy seed cake 92
*see also* makrut lime leaves
**loaf**
Brown butter loaf with brown butter frosting 100–1
Carrot, parsnip & cardamom loaf 77
Mandarin & bay leaf olive oil loaf 98
Seeded banana & pear loaf 96

**M**

**macadamia**
Chocolaty sweet potato & macadamia cream cake 86–7
macadamia vanilla cream 87
madeleines, Almond, mandarin & orange blossom 52
makrut lime leaves: Baked makrut lime & coconut rice pudding 132

**mandarin**
Almond, mandarin & orange blossom madeleines 52
Almond mandarin cake 74
Mandarin & bay leaf olive oil loaf 98
**mascarpone**
Chocolate, beetroot & orange cupcakes 48
Creamy raspberry & orange tart 126
Lemon tart 124
orange and mascarpone topping 48
**matcha**
Coconut matcha cake with matcha cake pops 114–15
matcha cake pops 114
melting moments, Passionfruit cashew cream 32
**muffin**
Jam duffins 66
Spiced apple & cream cheese muffins 64

**N**

natural food colours 120
nectarines: Peach, nectarine & ginger crumble 135
**nutmeg**
Carrot cake with lemon cream cheese frosting 108–9
spice powder 58
Spiced pumpkin donuts 58
nuts *see* almonds, cashews, hazelnuts, macadamias, peanuts, pecans, pine nuts, pistachios, walnuts

**O**

**orange**
Chocolate, beetroot & orange cupcakes 48
Creamy raspberry & orange tart 126
Hazelnut sponge with roasted strawberries & ricotta 104–5
orange and mascarpone topping 48
Orange blossom–baked apples & pears 129
Peach, nectarine & ginger crumble 135
Rhubarb & apple pie 136
Rhubarb & strawberry crumble 141
roasted strawberries and whipped ricotta 104–5
Rosemary, hazelnut & orange biscotti 37
Orange blossom–baked apples & pears 129
**orange blossom water**
Almond, mandarin & orange blossom madeleines 52
Almond mandarin cake 74
Orange blossom–baked apples & pears 129

## P

pandan: Coconut & pandan crème brûlée 130
parsnips: Carrot, parsnip & cardamom loaf 77
**passionfruit**
    Hummingbird cake 95
    Hummingbird layer cake with pineapple flowers 116–17
    passionfruit cashew cream 32
    Passionfruit cashew cream melting moments 32
**pastry**
    almond pastry crust 124, 126
    Gluten-free rough puff pastry 146–7
Peach, nectarine & ginger crumble 135
**peanut**
    Chocolate layer cake with peanut butter frosting 110–11
    peanut brittle 110
    peanut butter cheesecake base 83
    Peanut butter cookies 17
    Peanut butter frosting 151
    Peanut butter swirl cheesecake 83
**pear**
    Orange blossom–baked apples & pears 129
    Pear & chocolate frangipane galettes 69
    Seeded banana & pear loaf 96
peas: Baked vanilla & pea donuts 60
**pecan**
    Brown butter pecan shortbread fingers 23
    Carrot cake with lemon cream cheese frosting 108–9
    Peach, nectarine & ginger crumble 135
pepitas see pumpkin seeds
pepperberries: Cracked pepperberry shortbreads 26
pie, Rhubarb & apple 136
pine nuts: Rosemary, hazelnut & orange biscotti 37
**pineapple**
    Hummingbird cake 95
    Hummingbird layer cake with pineapple flowers 116–17
pistachios: Baked vanilla & pea donuts 60
polenta: Crunchy lemon myrtle & polenta shortbread 29
popcorn: Chocolate layer cake with peanut butter frosting 110–11
poppy seeds: Sweet potato, lime & poppy seed cake 92
prunes: Fig, prune & cranberry crumble slice 57
pudding, Baked makrut lime & coconut rice 132
**pumpkin**
    Pumpkin & fennel scones 83
    pumpkin seeds: Seeded banana & pear loaf 96
Spiced pumpkin donuts 58
purée, Apple 148

## Q

quinoa: Peach, nectarine & ginger crumble 135

## R

Rainbow cake 120–1
**raspberries**
    Coconut raspberry jam slice 45
    Creamy raspberry & orange tart 126
    Jam duffins 66
    Raspberry chia jam 149
**Rhubarb**
    Rhubarb & apple pie 136
    Rhubarb & strawberry crumble 141
**rice**
    Baked makrut lime & coconut rice pudding 132
    Peach, nectarine & ginger crumble 135
**ricotta**
    Baked lemon cheesecake 80
    Hazelnut sponge with roasted strawberries & ricotta 104–5
    roasted strawberries and whipped ricotta 104–5
roasted strawberries and whipped ricotta 104–5
Rosemary, hazelnut & orange biscotti 37
**rosewater**
    Almond, rosewater & chocolate donut cakes 46
    Hazelnut sponge with roasted strawberries & ricotta 104–5
    roasted strawberries and whipped ricotta 104–5

## S

scones, Pumpkin & fennel 83
Seeded banana & pear loaf 96
**sesame seeds**
    Chocolate layer cake with peanut butter frosting 110–11
    Coconut matcha cake with matcha cake pops 114–15
    Lime cheesecake tart 78
    matcha cake pops 114
    Tahini shortbread buttons 18
**shortbread**
    Brown butter pecan shortbread fingers 23
    Cracked pepperberry shortbreads 26
    Crunchy lemon myrtle & polenta shortbread 29
    Tahini shortbread buttons 18
**slices**
    Coconut raspberry jam slice 45
    Fig, prune & cranberry crumble slice 57
**sorghum**
    Gluten-free flour blend #2 (for cakes) 145

gluten-free flour pastry blend 146
    Gluten-free rough puff pastry 146–7
**spice mixes**
    spice powder 58
    cinnamon powder 68
Spiced apple & cream cheese muffins 64
Spiced pumpkin donuts 58
**spinach**
    natural food colours 120
    Rainbow cake 120–1
squash see pumpkin
**star anise**
    Banana chai blondies 42
    Chai chia cupcakes 51
**strawberry**
    Hazelnut sponge with roasted strawberries & ricotta 104–5
    Lime cheesecake tart 78
    Rhubarb & strawberry crumble 141
    roasted strawberries and whipped ricotta 104–5
**sunflower seeds**
    Lime cheesecake tart 78
    Seeded banana & pear loaf 96
**sweet potato**
    Chocolaty sweet potato & macadamia cream cake 86–7
    Sweet potato, lime & poppy seed cake 92
swirl, coconut–date 40
Swiss meringue buttercream 152
syrup, citrus 90

## T

Tahini shortbread buttons 18
**tarts**
    Creamy raspberry & orange tart 126
    Lemon tart 124
    Lime cheesecake tart 78
    Tarte Tatin 138
Tarte Tatin 138
Toasted almond, coconut & chia cookies 20

## V

**vanilla**
    Almond, mandarin & orange blossom madeleines 52
    Baked lemon cheesecake 80
    Baked makrut lime & coconut rice pudding 132
    Brown butter pecan shortbread fingers 23
    Cookies & cream blueberry cheesecake 84
    Passionfruit cashew cream melting moments 32
    Rhubarb & strawberry crumble 141

## W

walnuts: Carrot cake with lemon cream cheese frosting 108–9

# Acknowledgements

To the always fabulous Paul McNally: thank you so much for including me in your vision and for the opportunity to work with you and your mighty Smith Street Books.

There are always so many people that bring a book to life. Thank you Aisling Coughlan for keeping me in line, and to Lucy Heaver and Hannah Koelmeyer for your precision and editing expertise.

Big thanks to the talented shoot team: Chris Middleton for the beautiful images and Vicki Valsamis for your styling skill and creative eye. There would have been nothing to shoot if it weren't for the gorgeous Jemima Good – for all your hard work, keeping things moving in the kitchen and your food skills, thank you. For the fresh and striking new design, thank you Andy Warren. Thanks to Megan Ellis for the layout and Eugenie Baulch for proofreading.

Thanks and love to family, friends and neighbours for taste-testing along the way (and over the years), and for your valuable feedback. I am proud to be the 'crazy cake lady from over the road!'.

I would not be able to create and spend my time doing what I love without the incredible support of my wonderful husband Kaine. You keep our world turning and on track. You, along with our beautiful boys, are the greatest. I love you and thank you for putting up with me (and my noisy mixer).

Always, to my late parents, Doreen and Alan. I thank them for their tireless support and confidence in me from the very beginning.

Finally, thank you to you, for purchasing this book. I sincerely hope that you bring joy to your loved ones with treats from these pages.

# About the Author

Caroline Griffiths is a qualified home economist, cook, food writer, photoshoot chef and food stylist with a keen interest in nutrition. She is based in Melbourne, Australia. She is a passionate food expert with 20+ years of food-industry experience, having worked in several of Australia's best-loved test kitchens, including the *Australian Women's Weekly* and Dairy Australia. She has authored five cookbooks and contributed to dozens more.

Caroline loves to create recipes that are flavourful, wholesome, creative, achievable and, without question, delicious. When she's not trying to protect the family veggie patch from pesky possums, you'll find her spending time with family and her rapidly growing boys, experimenting in the kitchen or reading about food.

Published in 2023 by Smith Street Books
Naarm (Melbourne) | Australia
smithstreetbooks.com

ISBN: 978-1-9227-5414-1

All rights reserved. No part of this book may be reproduced or transmitted by any person or entity, in any form or means, electronic or mechanical, including photocopying, recording, scanning or by any storage and retrieval system, without the prior written permission of the publishers and copyright holders.

Copyright text © Caroline Griffiths
Copyright photography © Chris Middleton
Copyright design © Smith Street Books

Publisher: Paul McNally
Senior Editor: Lucy Heaver
Photographer: Chris Middleton
Stylist: Vicki Valsamis
Food preparation: Caroline Griffiths
Food assistant: Jemima Good
Project editor: Aisling Coughlan
Designer: Andy Warren
Typesetter: Megan Ellis
Indexer: Helena Holmgren
Proofreader: Eugenie Baulch

The publisher would like to thank The Establishment Studios, Melbourne, for the use of the props and surfaces used throughout this book.

The recipes in this book were originally published in *Incredible Bakes* in 2016.

Colour reproduction by Splitting Image Colour Studio
Printed & bound in China by C&C Offset Printing Co., Ltd.

Book 247
10 9 8 7 6 5 4 3 2 1